Analyse Yourself

A teen's guide to understanding their friends,
parents, and themselves!

Analyse Yourself

A teen's guide to
understanding
their friends, parents,
and themselves!

Karyn Gordon

CASTLE QUAY BOOKS
CANADA

Analyse Yourself
A teen's guide to understanding their friends, parents and themselves!

Copyright © 2002 by YACKA *Productions Inc.*

Printed in Canada

International Standard Book Number: 1-894860-00-4
Second Printing, March 2003

Published by:
Castle Quay Books
1740 Pilgrims Way, Oakville, Ontario L6M 1S5
Tel: 1-800-265-6397   Fax (519) 748-9835
Email: *info@castlequaybooks.com*
www.castlequaybooks.com

National Library of Canada Cataloguing in Publication Data

Gordon, Karyn, 1973-
    Analyse yourself : a teen's guide to understanding their friends, parents and themselves!

Includes bibliographical references and index.
ISBN 1-894860-00-4

    1. Self-esteem in adolescence. 2. Teenagers—Conduct of life.
I. Title.

BJ1661.G67 2002   158.1'0835   C2002-900908-1

To Mom and Dad,
You watched me struggle and persevere as
a teenager, yet loved me enough
not to rescue me. Instead, you
encouraged me to take risks
and try new things. You
gave me room to grow. This
really built my self-esteem!
Thank you for believing in me when
I didn't believe in myself!
I've so appreciated your support
and wisdom!

To my dear friends, Lynette, Loreli & Marie,
You greatly shaped my attitude towards myself.
Thank you for being my lasting
"Lifer" friends and
continually challenging me!

To Brent,
You are one of my many treasures
in working towards a
healthy self-esteem!

I love you all!

TABLE OF CONTENTS

FIRST BASE: The Attitudes
What is your attitude?
What are the attitudes of your friends & parents?

SECOND BASE: The Impact
Why are the attitudes important?
How does your attitude impact your life?

THIRD BASE: The Steps

**How can you feel great about yourself?
How can you help others feel great
about themselves?**

HOME PLATE: The Rewards

What are the rewards of being a Lifer?

PREFACE

The first time I remember hearing about "self-esteem" was when I was 14 years old, in health class. My family and I had just moved to a town north of Toronto, and I started attending a **new** high school. Back then I was shy, observed much, but spoke little. It still amazes me today, the way I was. I now love to speak to crowds of teenagers as if I'd done it my whole life.

When I was in Grade Nine, I **envied** other students. I compared myself to them, and then felt really awful about myself. Stephanie was one person whom I envied and of whom I thought, *This girl has her act together and the perfect life.* She was beautiful, thin, perfectly made-up, had designer clothes, was a straight-A student and was admired by all the guys who saw her. What more could a girl want? To most people, Stephanie had it made, or at least it appeared that way.

My life seemed just the opposite. I was certainly not beautiful and very shy, struggling with a learning disability. I received low marks despite studying a lot. I also wore second-hand clothes since my family was not wealthy.

Ironically, later in high school Stephanie and I became friends. I remember feeling really privileged to be her friend. However, over time, I became aware of a shockingly different side of her. This "so- perfect" girl was suffering from depression, had an eating disorder, had tried to commit suicide in high school, and frequently said, "I wish I felt better about myself."

I didn't get it! This new discovery made no sense to me.

How could someone who appeared so perfect on the outside be falling apart on the inside? Many questions whirled around in my mind. What I had learned about one's views about oneself in health class did not answer my questions. All I'd learned was the textbook definition of self-esteem. "Self-esteem is . . . blah, blah, blah!" So what? That didn't give me any answers!

I wanted to understand Stephanie's problem. If I had known then what I know now, I would have realised that not only did Stephanie struggle with low self-esteem, but I did as well. The only difference was that Stephanie expressed her low self-esteem frequently, and I was unaware of mine.

The desire to understand human behaviour motivated me to study psychology at university. Further graduate studies in counselling taught me how human behaviour can be changed. I began to understand that one of the most valuable things one can do for oneself is to learn about self-esteem and get a grip on our attitude towards ourselves.

Please note that although the stories in this book are true, in many cases I have changed names and locations to ensure confidentiality.

INTRODUCTION

Before we look at what self-esteem is, let's look at what it's not!

Myths about Self-Esteem

* We're born with it.   **False!**
* We can't control it.   **False!**
* If our parents put us down, it's
  impossible to have it.   **False!**
* If we're smart, good-looking, wealthy,
  wear the right clothes, date the right
  person, drive the right car, have
  the right job, hang out with the
  right people—we'll naturally get
  healthy self-esteem.   **False!**

Truths about Self-Esteem

* It's an attitude that we've learned.   **True!**
* We choose our self-esteem.   **True!**
* We can control how we
  think about ourselves.   **True!**
* It takes time to gain a
  truly healthy self-esteem.   **True!**
* It's always possible to feel
  good about ourselves.   **True!**

The Quick Fix

Feeling truly happy about ourselves is not achieved by external things such as how good-looking we are, how smart we are, whether we come from a rich family, how much money we have or whether we wear the right clothes. These things make up the **Quick Fix**-a surface and temporary solution. It's only a matter of time before the "inferior feelings" come alive. My friend, Stephanie, focussed most of her attention on these sought-after utopian trappings. They made her feel good about herself for a length of time, but deep down, she did not feel better about herself.

Inside-Out

For the record, there is nothing wrong with being beautiful, smart, rich or having nice clothes. **But . . . are these things a solid base for anyone's self-esteem?**

If all these "things" disappeared - would your self-esteem vanish? If yes, you probably are dreaming about trying to achieve EXTERNAL "things" to feel good about yourself. It's much more realistic to start Inside-Out-work on liking the real you! And that's what this whole book is about! As one teen I interviewed strongly stated, "Forget about the hair, and the makeup. Concentrate on your inner self first, and the rest will come later!"

It's an Attitude

Self-esteem is an attitude, an opinion of ourselves that we have chosen to believe. Whether consciously or otherwise, we choose and control our attitudes, and these attitudes are then translated into feelings. For example, if I think I'm stupid, then I will feel stupid and inferior. I have been challenged on this idea by teens who question, "What about people who are told every day that they are worthless?" My response to this is that regardless of what we hear, we always have a choice what to believe about our-selves. (I'll address verbal abuse in a later chapter).

The great news is that because it's an **attitude** that we have chosen, we can choose to change it. We are not stuck with it for the rest of our life. This means that we all have the power to feel genuinely good about ourselves! Of course, this is a process, and it takes time and energy, but it is possible! Now some of us just need to learn how.

So far, I haven't told you any more about self-esteem than my health class teacher taught. She talked to us about self-esteem while our entire class, myself included, yawned, rolled our eyes and thought, "This is a drag!" She really missed the point by failing to explain the most important elements of all! There are lifetime rewards for having an honest, healthy understanding of ourselves, and crummy consequences if we don't.

If you can visualize self-esteem as a baseball diamond, this book will run you through the three Bases to Home Plate. At First Base, we'll be assessing ourselves and the key question is "**What.**" What are the attitudes? What kind of attitude do you currently have? How about your parents and friends? I'll talk about the different attitudes and kinds of self-esteem we commonly see. At Second Base we'll examine **Why** self-esteem is so important. We'll see the impact that self-esteem has on all areas of our life and hopefully, you'll be motivated to work hard at getting rid of unhealthy attitudes. Third Base is "**How.**" How can we **feel great** about ourselves? Third Base addresses the choices and describes five strategies for getting a grip on your life and your self-esteem! By the time we reach Home Plate, you'll be ready to enjoy the victory of a personal home run. Just like the game, it takes work, discipline and time, but the rewards are great!

As you begin to read this book, I want to challenge you to do something very courageous. Take a really honest look at yourself. Where are you right now in regard to your self-esteem? Where do you want to go? Drop everything and start evaluating yourself by taking the time to really get to know yourself! It's an investment with short and long-term rewards that are well worth it.

Hopefully, by the end of this book, you'll have a positive, uplifting and motivating understanding of yourself. You might even start looking at the people around you and begin to **UNDERSTAND** why they act in a certain way and say certain things. Then, congratulate yourself! You will have learned how to get a grip on your life!

FIRST BASE

The Attitudes

- WHAT IS YOUR ATTITUDE?
- WHAT ARE THE ATTITUDES OF YOUR FRIENDS & PARENTS?

CLAIM YOUR ATTITUDE
AND BLUEPRINT

THE BLIND (low self-esteem)

* may put themselves down
* may hear negative comments ("You're worthless") and believe them ("I'm worthless")
* may feel less important than other people
* may know their weaknesses, but not their strengths
* may feel they have little worth or value
* may expect put-downs from others
* may believe and accept negative comments from others
* may focus on their mistakes and weaknesses
* may believe they have to be perfect
* may fear future situations and avoid change

"When people feel they have little worth, they expect to be cheated, stepped on, and depreciated by others. This opens the way to becoming a victim. Expecting the worst, these people invite it and usually get it. To defend themselves, they hide behind a wall of distrust and sink into the terrible feeling of loneliness and isolation. . . . Fear is a natural consequence of this distrust and isolation. Fear constricts and

17

blinds us; it keeps us from risking new ways of solving problems. . . . Much of what happens to us is the outcome of an attitude. Since it is an attitude, we can change it."[i]

In Grade 10, I remember changing after gym class and listening to classmates' comments. . . . "I'm fat"; "I need to lose weight"; "I'm going to fail the science exam like always." Negative comments about themselves poured out of their mouths. Were they all true? No! Many were **lies**. So why did they put themselves down so frequently? Many of us choose to be blind, wallowing in low self-esteem. When I was in Grade 9, I chose to be blind. I thought I had no choice.

The Blind don't see the truth. They choose not to see their strengths, capabilities and the positives in their life. They too often focus on their "curses" instead of their "blessings." The Blind often complain to friends about their "many imperfections" and desperately seek affirmations in return. If you ask them, "What are your strengths?" they often say, "I don't have any." In reality, we are each endowed with certain strengths. Unfortunately, the Blind have a poor attitude towards themselves, feeling inferior to others.

My friend Stephanie was Blind, and to cure her inferior feelings she chose the "Quick Fix." She spent hours on her external image by losing weight, exercising, and studying many hours to get an A average. She failed to get to know the real Stephanie. Who was she? In spite of the looks, the marks and the guys–Stephanie still felt like "**A NOTHING**." She only briefly felt confident when she perfected her outward appearance. As I mentioned earlier, the "Quick

Fix" works only if everything goes well! But, if the boyfriend dumps you, you gain weight, or you do poorly on an exam, depression often sets in.

Choosing Blindness has many consequences in other parts of your life, which I'll address at Second Base, the Impact.

THE DISGUISED (false self-esteem)
* may put others down
* may externalise negative comments ("You are worthless")
* may act superior to other people
* may appear overly confident and arrogant
* may deny that they have low self-esteem, but in reality they truly have it

---

During my University days, I had a part-time job working as a secretary for a packaging company. Elaine, a sales rep, was one woman I unfortunately had to work with. Her behaviour towards me was often malicious. She would come in and verbally berate me. "I hate your hair. Why do you wear those clothes? This package looks like garbage." I would always cringe when she walked towards my desk, anticipating negative comments. She appeared so confident, acting as if she were better than everyone in the office. I felt that she wanted to rip me to pieces with her verbal attacks. I'm sure we all have met an Elaine at some point in our life.

During my psychology classes, I learned why people like Elaine put others down. Those like Elaine are Disguised, and have false self-esteem. Understanding about false self-esteem was a "gift from above," because it helped me understand her and stopped me from believing her comments.

The Disguised are wearing masks. They appear extremely confident and arrogant, often putting other people down. Why? Because they feel insecure. They put others down to elevate themselves. They want other people to feel as poorly as they do. While the Blind feel inferior to others, the Disguised act superior, but actually feel like the Blind. But, unlike the Blind who openly share their imperfections, the Disguised usually deny any "flaws" about themselves. The Disguised can be as **blunt** as Elaine, saying, "I hate what you're wearing," or can be subtle by making negative comments about others to a third party–back stabbing. The bottom line is that the Disguised appear as though they are confident, but deep inside they feel depressed or unhappy about themselves, just like the Blind.

I realised that my co-worker, Elaine, was putting me down because she didn't feel so great about herself. She wanted to put me down continually, so I would feel inferior. When I realised this, I thought, "I'm not going to believe her comments." I realised Elaine wanted to make me angry, so that I would blow up and perhaps get fired. Then who would have lost **CONTROL**? Me! So I acted exactly the opposite of what she wanted–I acted genuinely nice! When she put me down, I responded positively, or with a compliment. The nastier she got, the more compliments I gave her. Eventually my boss pulled me into her office and said, "Karyn, I've heard you're fighting with Elaine." I said, "She may have a problem with me, but I don't have a problem with her. When I first sensed that she was mad at me, I asked her if something was wrong, and she said no really quickly. I'm not a mind reader, so I didn't know what is going on in her head. All I know is that she continually puts me down, but that's her problem. Just listen this week to how she talks with me."

My boss decided to eavesdrop on our conversations for one week to understand how Elaine talked to me. She listened to get a picture of the whole situation: "Karyn, that dress does not suit you." My reply was, "Actually I love this dress, and your outfit looks great on you." She would huff and storm off. Within two weeks, Elaine was gone, either fired or perhaps strongly encouraged to quit, I don't really know which. I had learned how to not let Elaine push my buttons.

When living with, dating, or working with people who are Disguised, just remember—the comments that they project onto you are a reflection of how they view themselves! If they seem to hate you, it's because they actually hate themselves. But, unfortunately, you are the target! We'll talk later about how to respond to the Disguised and Blind.

THE FLIPPERS
(flip temporarily between false and low self-esteem)

* may put themselves or others down
* may feel inferior or act superior to other people
* may know their weaknesses, but not their strengths
* may feel they have little worth or value but may deny having low self-esteem
* may expect put-downs from others
* may internalise negative comments ("I'm worthless") or externalise negative comments ("You're worthless")
* may believe and accept negative comments from others
* may focus on their mistakes and weaknesses
* may fear future situations and don't like change

21

You might know someone in-between the Blind and Disguised. Perhaps they are Flippers. Flippers go between putting themselves and other people down. It's easy for this to happen, since the Blind and Disguised feel the same way. However, although they have similar feelings, they act out differently! While the Blind internalise negative comments, "I'm worthless," the Disguised externalise their comments, "You're worthless." The Flippers flip in-between, saying "I'm worthless and you're worthless."

When I first started my counselling practice, I counselled a shy 14-year-old named Susan who struggled with Blindness. She put herself down, called herself worthless and felt she was created without any gifts. Most of our brief counselling time focussed on building up her self-esteem, highlighting her strengths, challenging her negative thoughts, setting personal goals and facing her fears. She made a lot of progress. Two years later, I saw Susan again. I couldn't believe it was her. She was loud, **arrogant** and conceited, cutting people off in their conversation. I realised she had merely flipped from being Blind to being Disguised. This sometimes happens when we're trying to build ourselves up. We overdo it and start putting other people down.

Some people, like Susan, change drastically from Blind to Disguised. Others flip temporarily, depending on the kind of day they're having. Nonetheless, they still feel inadequate on the inside.

THE LIFERS (healthy self-esteem)

* often feel equal to other people
* often know their *strengths*, and work to strengthen weak areas, or accept their weaknesses

* often feel they are unique, special and loved
* often choose what to believe from others
* often filter out negative comments
* often *learn* from their mistakes
* often take responsibility for themselves
* often face life with confidence and happiness

"Integrity, honesty, responsibility, compassion, love and competence-all flow easily from people whose self-esteem is high. We feel that we matter, that the world is a better place because we are here. We have faith in our own competence. We are able to ask others for help, yet we believe we are our own best resources. Appreciating our own worth, we are ready to see and respect the worth of others." [ii]

Since I was 15 years old, I have loved watching Oprah. Her talk show has made a real impact on my life and how I view myself. She is one of my role models, a person whom I aim to be more like. Why? Because she chose to be a Lifer. She is truthful about herself, shares her various struggles and challenges, dismisses negative comments from the media, and acknowledges her strengths. She builds others up and rarely puts herself down. She seems to have a strong understanding of who she is, showing a healthy liking for herself.

The Lifers know their strengths and work to strengthen weak areas, or accept their weaknesses. They view themselves as equals with others-so there is no motivation to put themselves or others down. Why waste time and energy putting someone down? The Lifers take responsibility for their life and their decisions! They set realistic personal goals and strive towards them. If they reach the goal, they celebrate! If not, they know they've tried their best! When they hear a negative comment, they don't automatically believe it. They filter the comment by asking themselves, "Who said this? Is it true? Should I believe this comment? What can I do about this? What are my choices?" This filtering process, called positive cognitive thinking, is an art and well-worth developing! The Lifers are confident and happy about who they are.

This serenity prayer, the Lifers know all too well:

"God, grant me the serenity to **accept** the things I cannot change,
courage to change the things I can,
and the wisdom to know the difference."

When I was 15 years old, I wanted to be a confident Lifer, but I just didn't know how. It's taken 10 years for me to truly understand how! Remember, being a Lifer is a choice and an attitude, and it's always possible. Third Base will show us how.

SECOND BASE

The Impact

- WHY ARE THE ATTITUDES IMPORTANT?
- HOW DOES YOUR ATTITUDE
  IMPACT YOUR LIFE?

Since self-esteem is my attitude about myself, it represents the <u>core</u> of who I am. This attitude impacts every area of my life. This base will show you how.

UNDERSTAND THE POTENT IMPACT OF YOUR SELF-ESTEEM

The first thing I want to mention is that we often choose friends who are emotionally similar to us. For example, if you are Blind or Disguised you might notice that most of your friends are Blind or Disguised. If you're a Lifer, most of your friends probably are as well.

FRIENDSHIPS:
The Blind & Disguised may

* be easily jealous
* be people-pleasers
* be self-focussed
* be dishin' it but not livin' it
* say "You're just saying that" when you give them positive comments because they are more likely to seek and accept negative comments[iii]
* back stab friends
* (girls), if hurt by their friends, be more **aggressive** (e.g., leaving friends out)
* (guys), if hurt by their friends, be more physically aggressive (e.g., fighting, punching)[iv]

Easily Jealous
I'll never forget one very disappointing conversation I

had with my good friend, Rachael. I was 22 years old and starting to present many motivational workshops to high school assemblies. The media caught on to my work, and I received a lot of media coverage, interviews on TV shows and in newspapers. When I shared this with Rachael, her first comment wasn't, "Karyn, I'm so proud of you." Instead, she said angrily, "That's not fair! How come nothing like that ever happens to me?"

I couldn't believe Rachael's response–instant **jealousy**! I was devastated. One of my closest friends couldn't be happy for me! She knew that I had spent 5 solid months trying to find one school that would allow me to speak. Getting started was really tough because I was so young. For months, all I heard from schools was rejection: "You're too young." One school bluntly told me, even after I offered it for free, "Try us again once you get some experience." What an insult! You offer your services for free, and someone still rejects you. Ouch! Besides, how can you get experience if you can't get started? I got so frustrated that I begged one high school to let me do a free workshop to 200 of their students, in exchange for a reference letter. They agreed. The workshop received great feedback. As a result, I got an excellent reference letter and 30 school bookings for the following month.

After all my hard work, why couldn't Rachael be happy for me? Because she chose to be Blind. Rachael had low self-esteem. She focussed on her **weaknesses**, and was Blind to her strengths. Because she was not satisfied with herself, she was easily jealous and found it difficult to be encouraging towards her friends. Getting discouraging responses is a major consequence of being in a friendship with someone with low self-esteem. I always believed friends were to be uplifting and encouraging, not discouraging. I had to re-evaluate how good this "good friend" truly was.

However, I have to admit I understood what Rachael was feeling because, when I struggled with low self-esteem, I continually compared myself with other people as well. As a result, I felt worse about myself back then.

People Pleasers

If the Blind don't act jealous, they may do the opposite and act as "People Pleasers." People Pleasers will basically do whatever you want, whenever you want and wherever you want. They want your approval, so if you ask for anything, they will usually say yes. As a result, People Pleasers are often taken advantage of, act like doormats, and as a result feel worse about themselves. They forget that it's OK to say no. Or they feel guilty if they say no. You can imagine how often People Pleasers get taken advantage of in dating relationships.

Don't get me wrong. Doing helpful things for other people is wonderful and rewarding. However, what's the motivation? Are you trying to get someone else's approval? To keep the peace? Do you genuinely want to help the other person? Make sure you are doing it for the right reasons!

Self-Focussed

Another consequence of being Blind is that they are often self-focussed. They sometimes act as if the world revolves around them. They are so overwhelmed by their own problems that they may find it difficult to ask about how someone else is doing. My friend Rachael talked continually about her "problems." I noticed early in our friendship that she seldom asked about how I was doing. If she did, it was at the end of the conversation, when we had little time left. On one occasion, I timed how long she talked about herself before she even asked how I was doing. Fifty-five minutes went by before I heard, "So, Karyn, how are you?" Just as I started to share some personal things, she said, "Oh, I'm sorry, but I have to go now." That's when I took a real hard look at our friendship. I found it very unbalanced and unsatisfying.

'Dishin' It But Not Livin' It'

After one of my high school workshops, two teenaged girls came up to me. They looked confused and frazzled. They said, "Karyn, everything you said about low self-esteem describes us. We put ourselves down, we don't think we have any strengths and we don't think we're pretty. We give great advice to each other. But we don't take our own advice." As I listened to them, I tried to imagine myself in their shoes, and a few things came to mind. If I was struggling with a problem, and I heard great advice, I probably wouldn't trust that information if I knew that the "source individual" didn't live by her own advice. People who don't practice what they preach have very little credibility with me. It's easy to talk, and difficult to live. We should never tell someone to do or say something that we ourselves wouldn't do or say.

That's why when I started doing self-esteem workshops with teens, I quickly learned to make myself vulnerable and share my own personal struggles with my audience. This helped me to gain credibility in the opinion of my audience.

Many times, after I spoke I had a line-up of teens, each one telling me, "Your personal story made me realise that it's possible to overcome self-esteem issues," and "Your story had the most impact on me." My audience trusted me because I was not asking teens to do something that I didn't actually do myself. When we say and live what we teach, it's called having integrity. Only then will people around us put their trust and confidence in us.

I observed these two teen girls feeding into each other's pattern of self-pity. Girl X would say, "I'm fat." Then Girl Y responded, "No, you're not, you've got a healthy body, but I'm fat." Then Girl X would say, "No, you're not fat. I am." This verbal pattern would be repeated over and over again. Their problems were self-pity and lack of high self-esteem. These girls were dependent on someone else to affirm them. It's as if each felt their self-esteem was in the lap of their friend. The bottom line is that we need to take our self-esteem and put it in our own lap–we own it!

Were the girls actually helping each other? A "Quick Fix" comment and the attention of their friend was the short-term reward. But long-term, did the girls actually feel better about themselves? They both said no, because they did not believe the positive comments made by each other.

These girls were dependent on their friend's affirmations, and they sought their self-esteem externally! Instead of starting with themselves and looking at who they are, they complained hoping to get a quick compliment. If we rely solely on other people's comments, we are in a dangerous and "no-win" situation. Someone else is completely controlling our self-esteem. What a vulnerable feeling. <u>We need to look "Inside-Out" and begin to own our self-esteem</u>.

"You're Just Saying That"

Do you know anyone who downplays your positive comments? For example, you say, "You're great at getting along with people." And they respond, "You're just saying that."

The parents of a teenaged boy, Peter, came in to see me. Peter was Disguised and they knew he **struggled** with self-esteem. The parents were trying to build him up by giving some positive comments. Peter's response was, "Yeah, right," or "You're just saying that because you're my mom." His parents were frustrated and hurt. His dad told me, "I feel so discouraged, so I have stopped saying anything positive to him."

As a result of Peter's arrogant attitude, his self-worth remained at a low level. Peter was Disguised. He put down other people so they would feel hurt, because he couldn't handle compliments that might change his self-evaluation. His insecurity resisted outside help.

The Disguised **PROJECT** onto others how they feel about themselves. Peter's comment to his dad sounds mean, and it is. But Peter probably tells himself this comment all the time, "Yeah, right. Life will get better." Peter's pain was deep and it came out directed at his parents.

As a friend, it can be frustrating to share positive comments with the Disguised. If you think that all your comments are being "stomped on," you might withdraw from the friendship.

Although Peter's attitude pushed his dad away, deep down I think Peter desperately wanted to hear more, but he didn't know how to show it. I told his dad, "You cannot control whether Peter believes your comments or not, and it's not your responsibility to make sure he does believe them. But as a parent, it's your **responsibility** to tell him. If he puts you down again, tell him how his comments make you feel sad, and that it discourages you from saying anything more that is positive. But let him know that that is his choice."

So, the next week Peter's parents came back to see me. Sure enough, Peter's dad had told Peter, "I love you." As expected, Peter had responded, "Whatever." His dad had firmly said, "It frustrates me and hurts me when you respond that way. I can't make you believe something. But it is true. I do love you. And only I know my own feelings. It's not your right to tell me whether or not I love you. You can't read my heart and mind, and if you choose not to believe it, then that's your choice. I will continue to make positive comments to you, but if you keep responding this way, I will decrease them. But again, how you respond is your choice!"

Peter had huffed and walked away after his dad poured out his heart. Did anything change? Yes. The next time his dad said something positive, Peter stared back, as if not believing him, but he did stop the "yeah, right" comments. Individual counselling might have further helped Peter to overcome his negativity.

Friends that Back Stab

One of my counselling clients, 18-year-old Rebekah, came in to see me regarding her depression. She was feeling really low after she and her best friend, Cindy, got into a huge war of words. The fight turned *malicious* when Cindy started telling nasty rumours about Rebekah around their high school and threatened to kill her.

Rebekah, bawling her eyes out in my office, said, "Karyn, I don't know how a person could change like that.

She was my best friend." I was puzzled. I don't believe anybody changes overnight. Most often, there are **signs** in others that we overlook or pretend not to see. I asked Rebekah a lot about her friendship with Cindy. Rebekah admitted that Cindy was "kind" to her, but often back stabbed other people indirectly. For example, Cindy often gave Rebekah put-downs about their other friends. Rebekah said to me, "I knew she was mean to other people, but I didn't think she <u>could</u> be mean to me."

My advice is to be aware and on your guard when you see a negative pattern! If someone is comfortable back stabbing your friends, chances are he or she will back stab, or already has back stabbed **you**–because that person has chosen to be Disguised! The only way that individual knows how to feel better about himself/herself is by putting other people down. And until he or she learns how to gain a genuinely healthy self-image, that person will probably continue to act this way. Again, counselling may afford a change of heart for teens like Cindy.

If enough people pull away from and ignore the back stabber, maybe he/she will learn to change his/her behaviour. The problem is that people are often afraid of such an individual, fearing that he/she will "turn" next on them.

FRIENDSHIPS:
The Lifers

* are often positive towards themselves and others
* usually **choose** friends who are also Lifers
* are more likely to accept compliments and positive feedback from people because they believe the comments[iv]

Positive Towards Themselves and Others

We've learned that the Lifers view themselves as equals with other people. They try to act positively towards themselves and other people. Doesn't that sound like a Webster's Dictionary definition? But it is true! When I choose friends, I'm attracted to Lifer friends, who are secure within themselves, so they can affirm my strengths while challenging my weaknesses.

But if we want to gain good friends, we have to learn how to be a good friend ourselves! The famous verse, "Do unto others as you would want them to do unto you" (Matthew 7:12) is a wise statement, quite appropriate in our times.

I've had many friends, but my friend for the longest time has been Lynette. Lynette and I have been best friends since I was 4 years old. The cool thing is that Lynette and I are polar opposites–ask any one of our friends. I like getting dressed up, she's totally casual; I'm talkative, she's quiet; I love change and adventure, she prefers simplicity and routine; I wanted a career, she wanted to be a wife and mother. And yet, despite our differences, there has been a very strong common thread–loyalty and trust! Lynette knows me better than anyone else–and does not shy away from constructively challenging me if she thinks I'm in the wrong!

I mentioned earlier that there are many blessings to having a healthy self-esteem, and having truthful friendships is one of them. Generally, because you're positive to others, view them as equals and value their opinions, the Lifer people want to be around you.

As I said earlier, it's interesting that we choose friends who have a **SIMILAR** self-esteem to ours. For example, the Blind often have Blind or Disguised friends. Think about it for a moment and see if I'm right.

The Blind put themselves down, and the Disguised will put the Blind down. It's a perfectly unhealthy and destructive match. How ironic!

You'd think that the Blind would want a Lifer friend, but is such a friendship balanced? Remember, I said the Blind are often jealous of anyone's success and tend to be self-absorbed. On the other hand, the Lifer friend gives encouragement and often wants encouragement back. So, often, the Lifer friends want a Lifer friend in return. Having a Lifer friend is one of the many blessings of gaining a healthy self-esteem!

The Lifer's Friends

When I was in Grade 9, struggling with my low self-esteem and Blindness, I had two close friends who were Disguised! They often put other people down through sarcasm. I noticed that I'd started picking up the habit. I have to admit, putting people down was a "Quick fix" for my **feelings** of low self-worth. I didn't realise that my choice of Blind and Disguised friends was just an extension of myself. I chose Disguised friends because I was Blind.

However, in Grade 10, enough was enough and I started getting my life together with healthy self-esteem. I remember thinking, "I want to find new, kinder friends." So I started to socialise with different people. Of course, this caused conflict with my old friends, but it was a risk worth taking. I was tired and **exhausted** by the put-downs, and I knew that my "friends" would soon be putting me down as well. I wanted to upgrade myself and change. One of my first steps towards choosing to be a Lifer was to find some Lifer friends. But I had to start working on myself and move towards being a Lifer to attract other Lifer friends. This was a gradual process.

Dear Karyn,

I had a best friend, and we had a serious fight. This girl asked for his number, and they started going out. He started ignoring me 'cause of this girl, so I didn't talk to him for a week just to see if he'd notice or not. But he never called or e-mailed me. Then finally, I called him to see what he was doing, and he's like, "Oh, who's this?" and then he handed the phone to the girl, who wouldn't let me talk to my friend. I got so mad at him 'cause he always does this: whenever someone is around, he ignores me like he doesn't know me. So I paged him and said, "It's over! We are not friends anymore, and I'm not interested in talking!" For three or four weeks he never called, but later he e-mailed me some crap that really hurt.

I always considered him my best friend and all he did was treat me like s***. Honestly, I was always there for him no matter what. I never want to lose him as a friend, and I know I can't let him go.

Please tell me what I should do now. Obviously, I am not going to talk to him anymore, but still I want to know if I should reply with a nasty e-mail or should I just stay away?

Later,
Confused

Dear Confused,

We tend to use this word "friend" so loosely that we often forget what it means. True friends build you up, encourage you towards your goals and challenge you! "True friends" do not put you down, call you names, or ignore you. But if we expect true friendship from our friends, we'd better be a true friend ourselves. Friends truly are a mirror of ourselves!

Think first about whether this "friend" is worth investing time and energy in. You mentioned that he often ignores you when someone is around. Is this a true friend? You said you never want to lose him as your friend and that you "can't let him go." Why not? I'm not saying that moving on is easy, but is it better for you? The word "can't" is paralysing and, in this case, untrue. The truth is, it's up to you whether or not to keep this guy as your friend.

You have basically three choices to deal with this situation: 1) You could be aggressive, tell him off, scream out your anger. But in response, he'll probably get defensive and scream back at you, and the conflict will escalate. 2) You could be passive, and avoid the whole situation, but then the conflict is not getting resolved and you're not sticking up for yourself. 3) You could try the assertive approach, which is the most effective and definitely the most mature!

To be assertive, state your feelings, using the word "I," and explain your feelings. (For example, "I felt really hurt because it seemed to me like I was being ignored.") In this example, you're talking about yourself, so people are more likely to listen. If you change the sentence to "You" (for example., "You make me so mad"), it's an attacking statement that would make most people react defensively.

The reason I focus on feelings is because it's a safe place and it speaks the truth! Talking about opinions ("I think that . . .") is not a safe place. Opinions are up for debate. Feelings are not. If someone says, "Oh, you shouldn't feel that way," it's an unfair statement. That's like telling a paralysed man that he should just get up and walk. What we feel is not in our control, but how we express our feelings is. The more you state your feelings, the more you're validating yourself and building your self-esteem.

When you're being assertive, it's critical to own your part of the situation. You are not responsible for his actions, but you are responsible for your 50 percent of this relationship. Be honest with yourself-is there anything you did that was not "true friend" behaviour? Did you yell, scream, or swear at him when you were angry?

Before you bring up your feelings, apologise for any behaviour that was unkind. This may seem extremely tough, but wouldn't you want him to do the same? Be the friend you want to have.

Being assertive is not easy, but in my opinion, that's how "true friends" handle conflict. It deals with the issue, validates your feelings, and often brings friends even closer.

Good luck!
Karyn[vi]

Published in the national Canadian magazine *What*, October 2000.

SECOND BASE: The Impact
How does your attitude about yourself affect your body language?

What does your self-esteem look like?

I never understood the power of body language until my trip to Israel . . .

Six years ago, I had an incredible opportunity to travel to Israel for 2 weeks on an historical biblical tour and archaeological excavation. One

night, my friend and I decided to meet for coffee at our hotel restaurant at 11:00 p.m. I had arrived early and was sitting by myself, observing this unique middle-eastern atmosphere. The room was smoky and had a strong cigar odour. There were over twenty-five men, mostly businessmen sitting alone, looking around or reading the newspaper. I was the only female. I felt a little *uncomfortable,* but I thought my friend would be arriving shortly.

There were three British guys, in their mid-twenties, sitting at the table across from me. I could see them, but couldn't hear them. All I could do was read their body language. After the waiter left, these guys noticed that I was watching them. So I quickly turned away, but the eldest guy started talking to me. He **asked** me if I was alone, and I said I was waiting for my friend to arrive. We small-talked for a while, about Canada and England, and what brought us to Israel. I learned that these were three brothers from England touring around Israel-Derek (the eldest), John (in the middle) and Jeff (the youngest).

Derek asked me, "So, Karyn, what kind of work do you do?" I replied, "I'm a teen therapist." "You're a what?" he replied, in this arrogant tone of voice. I answered, "I'm a therapist-a counsellor for teenagers." He gave me the most disgusted look, then replied loudly, "Yeah, right, look at you, like you could know anything." I couldn't believe this guy-who did he think he was? Just as he said this, the twenty-five men in the room started to laugh behind their newspapers. They had heard our entire conversation. I was ticked off and embarrassed. The adrenaline was rushing through me. Then I did something that I had never imagined I could do. I got out of my seat, stood up and loudly replied, "Derek, is that a challenge?" "What do you mean?" he asked. I replied, "If you don't think I could know anything, let me analyse you."

At this time, the room was so quiet you could have heard a pin drop. Many of the men had put down their newspapers and were fully listening to our conversation. Derek was quiet, but his two brothers said, "Do it, Karyn. Analyse him." Derek looked at me, and perhaps under pressure said, "Yeah, OK. Go ahead, analyse me. What could you possibly say about me?"

I started. "OK, Derek. You **appear** confident. But I think you're actually the least confident. It seems that you build yourself up by putting other people down. I think you control others because you have lost control in your own life. I doubt you like commitment, in relationships or work, and 'marriage' probably isn't even in your vocabulary. It seems that you hold a lot of **anger.** Watching you relate with your brothers gives me the impression that you have a thick angry wall around you. I bet something happened that you never got over, that made you feel really sad, so you have built a thick wall around yourself to prevent anyone from coming close to you again. Inside, you're probably really upset, but your ego is too big to let anyone know. So you act all tough, controlling other people and putting them down. Inside, you're a real gem of a guy, but because you haven't dealt with some of the deep feelings inside you, you're falling apart. My guess is that when you're **depressed**, you drink.

It's your 'Quick Fix,' so lately you've been drunk a lot. Does that sound about right?"

I'll never forget that moment. Derek stared blankly at me. His two brothers in their cute British accent said, "Karyn, that's incredible! You've described him to a tee." Just then, this entire room of Israeli men started to clap; they had heard our conversation and were agreeing!

Body language is a very powerful tool for reading someone's self-esteem. When I was in Grad school, one of my professors told us that roughly 93% of communication is through body language (eye contact, tone of voice and gestures). Only 7% of communication is verbal. So naturally, how we feel about ourselves will be communicated, whether we realise it or not.

BODY LANGUAGE:
The Disguised may

* appear superior and intimidating
* have eye movement that looks around a lot (so that you feel unimportant)
* have "glaring" eye contact, communicating. "That's a stupid idea."
* "stare" to intimidate you
* seldom smile
* fold their arms, showing a defensive posture
* cut off other people when they are talking
* huff when someone else shares his/her opinion
* act like a "know-it-all", as if they have the answer for everything
* try to CONTROL other people by making decisions for them
* be sarcastic or use subtle put-downs

When talking with the Disguised, we often feel intimidated, and possibly put down. That is often exactly what the Disguised want-to elevate themselves and push others down.

Derek chose to be Disguised. He built himself up by putting people down-a sign of his own feelings of inadequacy. There were certain "signs" that indicated to me where he was at. First, I noticed that he ordered a drink for his youngest brother (Jeff, 22 years old), which I thought was strange. I found that controlling and **inappropriate**. Jeff tried to order for himself, but Derek cut him off and ordered for him. Even in their conversation, although I couldn't hear anything, I noticed that John tried to talk, and Derek interrupted him, making a statement that made Jeff, but not John, laugh. It was probably some kind of sarcastic put-down about John. I sensed some competitive vibes between Derek and John. John seemed to "have it together." He was very pleasant, smiled a lot, and seemed at peace with himself. So John would be an easy target for Derek to throw his put-downs at. John's "together-ness" might be a constant reminder to Derek of his own lack of "together-ness." It was evident that Derek dominated their conversation, emitting put-downs and controlling his brothers by pressuring them to drink.

BODY LANGUAGE:
The Blind may

* seem inferior and easily intimidated
* show little eye contact
* stare without facial expression (you may wonder if they're listening)
* seldom smile or have a continual "**fake**" smile (to be accepted by others)

* give **little** facial expression when another person is talking
* give little verbal feedback to what another person has just said
* lean their shoulders really forward, communicating lack of confidence
* **fiddle** with their hands
* fold their arms across their chest, showing a defensive stance
* keep their head down, communicating INSECURITY
* talk nonstop about themselves
* seldom talk-thinking that their opinion is not of value
* switch the topic back to *themselves*, when someone else is talking
* have a "shaky" voice

Jessica, 17 years old, came to see me early in my counselling career. She didn't like talking. As I mentioned earlier, only 7% of communication is verbal. So even if someone doesn't want to talk, I can paint a picture of the person based on their body language. I really challenged this theory with Jessica. Not only did she not talk, she rarely looked at me. She never smiled, held her hands on her lap, leaned her shoulders forward, and had eye contact anywhere but with me. All I knew from her mom was that she was having problems making friends at school. I would ask Jessica a question, and she would roll her eyes, huff and then give me a quick answer in reply. Her non-verbal language communicated to me that she didn't want to be there.

One session, I confronted her. "Jessica, your mom told me that you're struggling to make new friends. Is this true?"

She glared back, huffed and said, "Maybe." "Jessica, you haven't told me anything about yourself, and that's OK. Obviously you don't feel comfortable yet. But let me tell you what I understand about you so far. You don't seem confident about who you are. You seem really sad and possibly angry at the world. It seems that you don't want to be here. It also seems that you're holding back from being honest with yourself and me. Is this true?" She looked at me and didn't say anything. I continued, "I'll be totally honest with you. If you don't want to be here, then let's talk with your mom and stop your appointments. But, if it's true that you want to make some friends at school, you can start learning some tools here. I'm wondering if you communicate the same way with your classmates as you do with me. If you do, maybe this is the problem. Let me tell you how your **BODY LANGUAGE** makes me feel. I feel you hate me. You seem really irritated, slightly arrogant and not friendly. If I were at school with you, I would be pushed away by your manner. I wonder if other students feel this way as well."

Jessica looked at me the whole time I was sharing with her. I had caught her attention. So I continued, "I can tell there is a lot inside of you. You have a lot of pain and sadness buried, and as a result, you probably built these big walls so no more sadness could come in. But the walls have to come down! The sadness is trying to come out. I think deep down you want the walls to come down, to feel happy again and to invite other people in. Shutting yourself off is not giving you the chance to experience friendships. You are pushing people away. Jessica, maybe I'm totally out of line, but this is what I'm picking up from your body language. Am I right?"

46

She looked at me, this time without a glare, and said, "Yeah." At that moment, she did something she had never done before–she owned her responsibility for failure in building friendships. Before that, she had blamed the kids at school as being "mean and unfriendly." And maybe they were. But I think her body language was encouraging other kids to avoid her. Jessica committed to counselling and came for **6** months after that discussion.

I firmly believe that we were created to be inter-relational. We all need people around us. Some of us need more people than others. Deep down, Jessica wanted friends. She just didn't know how to make them. She also didn't know what she was doing to repel people from her. It became a vicious circle. When she felt bad about herself, her body language communicated, "Don't bother me." This pushed people away, refuelling her low self-esteem.

The time I spent with Jessica focussed on her uniqueness. What could she offer as a friend to people? Instead of focussing on "What can I get" she gradually asked, "What can I give?" This is a big step for someone who does not think they have much to give. Jessica and I worked on discovering what made her special, along with practical social skills such as body language.

The Blind have their own body language. I'm sure we all know someone who is Blind. To understand how they communicate, we don't focus on what they are saying, but rather on what they are not saying.

Of the many Blind people I have worked with, there are certain **similarities** in their body language. First, they rarely smile. They look sad on the outside, often because they are sad on the inside. Not smiling has its consequences. If they rarely smile, this often repels people from being their friends. How many people want to be friends with someone who is sad most of the time?

Second, they talk about themselves and rarely ask about how the other person is. Have you ever talked with someone who doesn't **stop** talking? Just because someone is talkative or, conversely, shy does not mean they have low self-esteem. However, again, look at their behaviour. When someone talks non-stop, this communicates that they don't value your opinion. They care only about their own. If they did care about your ideas, they would ask you about them.

The opposite of the non-stop talker is the shy person. Shyness, like anything else, can be healthy or unhealthy, depending on the motivation. There are some people who rarely speak because they don't feel their opinion is of much value. They view their opinions and thoughts as less important than other people's, and therefore I would call them Blind. All people have a right to speak and be heard, and be of equal value to everyone else. There are also, however, shy people who know their opinion is of importance, yet they **choose** not to speak. Instead, they keep their thoughts private. In this case, this SHY person may be a Lifer. There are many shy Lifers!

The final aspect of body language is how they talk and walk. The Blind often give off an "insecure" body language: head held low, hands fiddling, shoulders leaning forward, little eye contact with the person of contact, and little facial change when another person is talking. A person might even wonder if such people are listening. The consequence is that this sort of body language often does not attract friends. Think about it. If I'm talking with someone and they are not looking at me when I'm speaking, or seem fidgety, or give me

few facial expressions, I think, "They're not listening, and they don't value what I'm saying." It's many small gestures that will attract someone to another person or repel him.

Again, that's why it's so important that we start working on our own self-esteem first.

BODY LANGUAGE:
The Lifer may

* communicate EQUALITY
* smile frequently (real smiling-not fake)
* give PLEASANT facial expressions when talking
* give appropriate verbal feedback when listening
* feel comfortable with steady eye contact
* ask your opinion, showing they value your ideas, and not turn the conversation back to themselves
* disagree with your opinions, but respects them, and never puts you down
* keep their shoulders straight and held high, communicating confidence
* hold their head straight (but not too high), communicating security
* have their arms and hands relaxed, communicating interest in what you are saying
* have their voice relaxed, coherent and confident

When I was in GRADE 7, my mentor and role model was a girl named Petra, a Grade 12 student. Petra babysat me occasionally on weekends when my parents went away. It was the way that she communicated with me that showed me two things: She valued me as a person, and she valued herself. She "oozed" a healthy confidence that I dreamed of having.

Even though I was only 11 years old, she would ask my opinion about a variety of different things (school, TV, movies, friends, etc.). When I talked, she would look right at me, as though I had her undivided attention. She would frequently smile, and change her facial expression appropriately when I talked. When we went out for dinner, everyone got a "please" and "thank-you," including waiters and busboys. Because she viewed all people as equal to her!

Her body language was RELAXED. Her head was held high, but not so high that she seemed arrogant. Her shoulders were back. Her hands were by her sides and never fidgeting. She gave off a presence that showed she had peace with herself-and she did!

So how do we gain this confidence, this inner peace with ourselves? I remember in Grade 9, I had to do a presentation in front of my science class. I was petrified! I hated public speaking because my throat would go dry, my hands would get clammy, I would talk too fast, and my voice would shake. I would clearly communicate insecurity, suggesting that I didn't know what I was talking about.

I remember practising for my science presentation in my bedroom the night before. I thought to myself, If I were confident, what would I look like? How would I sound? What would my face look like? I pictured Petra public speaking in her high school. Then I tried to imitate her. This sounds weird, but in front of my mirror for a couple of hours, I practised the "new" me-the confident me. My hands were CALM, my voice was strong and I paced my talking. I tried to "act" confident, even though I wasn't. Could I really pull this off tomorrow? It was worth a shot. Science class rolled around. I was nervous, but not as much as I usually was under such circumstances. I kept picturing the "new" me. I couldn't believe it! It worked! I felt like an actress in a play, acting like this confident "new" person who was real! Not only did I receive a good mark on the presentation, but I also received excellent feedback from my friends and teacher. They listened to me. I caught their attention with this presentation. Those who speak well tend to capture their audience. What an irony-this confidence stunt actually built my confidence! Rehearsing difficult situations that are coming up can really help build self-esteem.

There are so many benefits to having the Lifer body language! First, people listen! Think about it! **How** someone communicates is more important than WHAT they say. Since

7 %
of communication is verbal language
What is the person saying?
What words are they using?

while

93%
of communication is non-verbal language
How is the person communicating?
What is their tone of voice?
Are they yelling or whispering?
Is there any EYE CONTACT?
Are their shoulders back?

Have you ever had a teacher who knows the content of the course, but their method of teaching is boring and dull? It's very difficult to learn, isn't it? As a result, people often tune out and don't pay ATTENTION. But have you ever had a teacher who is so excited about his or her subject that it just seems to come to life? The content (what) hasn't changed, but the communication style (how) makes all the difference.

Another perk to having the Lifer body language is that it attracts people! Consider for a moment – wouldn't you want to talk with someone who pays attention to you, who is genuinely interested in what you're thinking and asks you questions, someone who doesn't put you down or cut you off to talk about themselves? Most of us do!

SECOND BASE: The Impact

How does your attitude about yourself affect your Relationships and Dating?

RELATIONSHIPS & DATING:
The Blind may

* be on the "Hunt" (for a relationship), often causing others to become "Runners"
* feel "INCOMPLETE without a relationship"
* think "I'd be happy if . . . dated me"
* believe their happiness is based on whether the right girl or guy likes them
* feel their relationship is their "reason for living"
* go from relationship to relationship with few breaks in between
* think "Why would anyone want to date me?"
* be in a co-dependent relationship because not only do they WANT it, they NEED it

* "cover-up" (make up excuses) for his/her partner's behaviour
* be attracted to the Blind or Disguised as a partner
* be afraid to be single
* be easily **jealous**

I used to admire girls like Cortney, a girl in my grade, who continually had boyfriends. Ever since Grade 8, she always had one boyfriend after another. She was gorgeous, popular, outgoing, and naturally many guys were attracted to her. But she never had just one. She usually had another one on the back burner. That's right! She would DATE at least two guys at the same time. I think it was a challenge for her to see that they didn't find out about each other. As soon as one relationship ended, another started. Why? Because she didn't want a guy for a relationship. She needed a guy to make her feel "complete." Her self-esteem bucket was low, near empty, and she thought the only way to fill it up was with the love of a boyfriend.

By the end of high school, she was already talking about getting married to Garry, her 3-year boyfriend. Of course, he didn't know that she had dated four other guys during their relationship. What I didn't understand was–How could she think about getting married when she cheated on her boyfriend? But Cortney wasn't truly in love with Garry; she was in love with the "idea" of Garry.

For Cortney, Garry represented a security blanket, a guy who would be "forever" by her side. Her fears of being alone would disappear, or so she thought.

I knew it was the "IDEA" of getting married that Cortney loved, because when Garry and Cortney broke up after high school, Cortney soon started dating Jeff. Within only 1 month, she started talking about getting married to him. I don't think she really cared whom she married–just as long as she got married.

The Hunters & Runners

Since Cortney needed guys to "fill up her self-esteem bucket," she soon became dependent on them. The Blind behave similarly in relationships as in friendships. Cortney needed a lot of attention and therefore would become easily jealous if her boyfriend hung out with his guy friends or even talked to other girls. Her self-esteem bucket was **low,** and she needed guys to be around frequently to fill it. You can imagine how this would damage outside friendships.

Her "hunting" behaviour for her boyfriend's attention usually caused the guys to respond in the same way. Most became "**RUNNERS**" and eventually took off. Garry told me after they broke up, "I felt suffocated. I couldn't do anything by myself or with my guy friends without her freaking out on me. She wanted me only to hang out with her. But I can't do that anymore! I lost contact with all my close friends when I dated her."

> Generally, the more one hunts,
> "the more the other runs."

Co-Dependent

In my counselling practice, I've noticed that more often girls tend to "hunt," while guys tend to "run." But interestingly enough, many of Cortney's boyfriends were "hunters." In high school, I noticed a pattern with her choice of guys. Cortney was beautiful, and yet she often dated unattractive guys with "little personality." As I look back, I notice that most of her boyfriends commented to me that she was "the most beautiful girlfriend" they had ever had. To the guys, she was this "trophy," a **status** symbol, the girl you want to hold on to no matter what the cost. To be "popular" at school, you needed to have this beautiful girlfriend. They didn't want to lose her, and often became a doormat to her needs and demands. She "hunted" dependent guys who, in return, "hunted" her back. She chose guys who needed her just as much as she needed them. She needed their love, and they needed her as a "trophy," which turned their relationship into a co-dependent one. Co-dependent relationships often result when the Blind date other Blind or Disguised people.

The Doormat

I've mentioned a few consequences of being Blind in relationships, becoming hunters or runners and being co-dependent. The Blind may become a doormat if they are trying to please others. In friendships, I talked about the Blind being people-pleasers. They will do whatever it takes to get someone's **approval**. You can imagine how people-pleasers can get themselves in trouble in relationships. Tracy was one example.

Tracy was 14 years old when she came to see me. She was very troubled and depressed. She began to tell me her horrific story. "When I was 12 years old, I dated Shawn, this older guy who appeared to love me. He wanted to have sex, and I didn't really want to but thought I would lose him if I didn't give him what he wanted. I thought he would love me. I thought sleeping with him would make me feel better about myself. It didn't. So I gave this guy my virginity, and instead of loving me he dumped me within a month. I guess he'd got what he wanted. I was so depressed that I started drinking and using pot. It was my escape. I just didn't want to be here anymore."

Tracy was a "doormat" for Shawn. She gave one of the most special parts of herself to a guy who didn't care about her. She was so DESPERATE for love that she would do whatever it took to get it. As a result, she felt used and abused. She was saying to herself, "Why should any guy love me? I'm not lovable." Tracy was looking for external self-esteem.

RELATIONSHIPS & DATING:
The Disguised may

* "Hunt" for a quick fling or relationship
* "Count the Trophies"
* verbally deny feeling "INCOMPLETE without a relationship," yet actions might show otherwise (usually hunting after a girl or guy)
* believe their happiness is based on their dating the "right girl or guy"
* go from relationship to relationship with few breaks in between
* tell themselves "I'm so great–why limit myself to only ONE partner?"
* have more than one dating partner at the same time
* put down their partner (just as they do their friends)
* try to control their partner
* have a co-dependent relationship because they NEED this relationship, but they don't WANT it
* continually check people out by eyeing others up and down
* be attracted to the Blind
* try to "Sever Their Partners' Roots" (friends and family support)
* be easily jealous

The Blind and Disguised are very similar in how they behave in relationships. They both need a relationship, although the Disguised may deny this. The Disguised may verbally say, "No, I don't need anyone." Yet their **BODY LANGUAGE** communicates that they are hunters, searching for that quick fling or relationship.

Counting the Trophies

While the Blind might look for love in a long-lasting relationship, the Disguised might look for a short-term one and "Count their Trophies" (i.e., brag about how many girls/guys they've dated, kissed or slept with). Counting the Trophies is another way that the Disguised build themselves up. It communicates to themselves and other people, "Hey–I'm great because I slept with . . . this weekend!" If they really cared about their partner, they wouldn't tell an audience. Counting the Trophies is an external ego booster. But, this has consequences. First, they might not experience a really loving long-term relationship because they're more interested in the number of partners versus the quality of those relationships. Also, if a guy is Counting the Trophies and girls hear about it–BYE BYE! Most girls try to avoid being with guys who only want to use them to add to their "list."

Remember the Disguised guy I talked with in Israel, Derek? After I finished analysing him, he started sharing about some of his former relationships. He said that in his early twenties, he was engaged to this girl, but "She dumped me." He talked as if he was the victim. I asked him why she dumped him, and he said, "I couldn't CONTROL my pants," meaning, he cheated on her. She found out and called it off. He never got over it and now was bitter. I asked him if he'd ever been totally faithful with any his girlfriends. He said no. He admitted that having more than one girlfriend made him feel really powerful and in control. That day she broke up with him, he lost control of his love life, but started controlling another part of his life–drinking.

Don't think that all the Disguised are cheaters! But after my working with them, many Disguised have admitted that it's an "ego thing" to date or sleep with as many people as possible. This is definitely not an act of love! Love is selfless, while Counting the Trophies is completely selfish.

Attracted to the Blind

While the Blind are attracted to the Disguised, the Disguised are attracted to the Blind. My good friend, Darlene, unfortunately found this out firsthand. Darlene admits that after high school she wavered between being a Lifer or Blind. When she was 21 years old, she went to college and began dating Luke, a popular, extroverted guy. They seemed to have the "perfect relationship." He was OUTGOING, while she was shy. He was a leader, and she was supportive. Both Darlene and Luke appeared to be very happy.

Yet, I heard about a very different Luke from Darlene. He sounded like he was a Flipper–flipping between being Blind and Disguised. To his friends he was Blind, occasionally putting himself down. But to his girlfriends he was Disguised, controlling them by his NEGATIVE comments.

He would tell Darlene such things as "I don't like your nail polish," and she would stop wearing nail polish. "I would be more attracted to you if you lost 10 pounds," so she started dieting. "I don't like your friends Karyn and x,y,z," so there would be tension between Darlene and me. I think he didn't like me because I challenged Darlene about how she was responding to his "put-downs." Darlene once told me, "I think he feels threatened by you because you see right through him."

RELATIONSHIP PARTNER

FRIEND

Many blind and disguised will slowly
distance their friends when they have a
relationship partner. They place themselves
in a vulnerable position when they rely
on mainly one root to support them,
because if the relationship ends,
the teen often feels "worthless"
and believes that their "life" is "over."

Darlene and Luke were planning on getting married, and obviously this terrified me! My friend was planning to marry this guy who was emotionally destroying her! I didn't know what to do. Stay quiet and keep the peace, or VOICE my concerns and risk losing a friendship? There were many "red lights" I saw about Luke: his verbal put-downs; his controlling statements; his many female friends who were "just friends," according to Luke, but in reality were much more. I loved Darlene too much to watch her throw away her life with this guy. I decided to voice my concerns.

I have already shared that how we say something is more important than what we say. I kept this at the back of my mind, and when Darlene and I went out for coffee one day, I shared with her some of my concerns. I said, "Darlene, I know you really care for this guy, but I have to be honest. I'm terrified! He's telling you put-downs, and you're believing them! Your self-esteem used to be so much greater, and it seems empty now. I know your heart is telling you to marry him, but what is your head saying?"

She paused and said, "My head tells me that I can find someone better, that he pulls me down, and that I'll be unhappy for the rest of my life. But my heart tells me he will change. I love him, and we could have a wonderful marriage together." I took a deep breath and said to Darlene, "Listen to your head. Our hearts are wonderful, but they can be misleading. If our heart and head say the same thing, we know we are making the right decision." Darlene responded, "Karyn, it's hard! You're the only one of my friends who doesn't approve of my marrying Luke." This comment really hurt me, and yet I knew that some of Darlene's other friends did agree with me. They just weren't saying anything.

Sever Your Roots

Luke would constantly put down Darlene's body image and friends. He wanted her to feel bad about herself so that she would need him. Overt or subtle put-downs are the ways that people try to control us. And when we actually do sever our roots (i.e., distance ourselves and let go of friends), then we are putting ourselves in a very dangerous and vulnerable position.

After 4 1/2 years, Darlene finally called it QUITS. By this time, her self-esteem bucket was practically empty. Breaking up with Luke was her first step towards building herself up again. She needed to learn to love herself and strive towards being a Lifer. Once she was a Lifer, she was attracted to other Lifers, and the Lifers were attracted to her! She is now married to a wonderful guy who genuinely loves her!

RELATIONSHIPS & DATING:
The Lifers may

* be attracted to other Lifers
* not need a relationship, but may want one
* feel like a **whole** person
* have a full "Self-Esteem Bucket"
* truly love themselves
* feel CONTENT whether they are single or in a relationship
* have a genuinely "selfless love" towards their partner
* encourage and **CHALLENGE** their partner to strive for their goals and dreams
* have "Many Roots" of support from family and friends
* strive to be interdependent (have friends outside the relationship)
* have "together-time" and "personal-time"

61

* share similar interests with their partner but have their own personal interests
* trust their "HEAD and Heart," but listen more to their head
* make good decisions
* learn about themselves from their experiences

Whole People Meet Whole People

In relationships, our self-esteem becomes a BLUEPRINT for what we expect from others. A few years ago, I went out for dinner with one of my friends, Marie, and her boyfriend, Dennis. I was curious about their self-esteem and how it impacted their relationship. They'd been dating for 9 months, and I would call them both Lifers. I asked them to pick a number from 0 to 10 to rate how much they liked themselves, 10 meaning you are perfect, and 0 meaning you don't like anything about yourself. When they both answered "7 or 8," I wasn't surprised. As these friends did, we tend to choose partners with the same level of self-esteem. If we truly love ourselves, we expect someone to truly love us back.

While there are many consequences to being the Blind and Disguised, there are many **blessings** to being the Lifers. First, the Lifers don't need a relationship. They feel good about themselves with or without a relationship. Since they are not dependent on this relationship to be happy, they are less likely to be jealous or demanding.

The Self-Esteem Bucket Is Full

Second, the Lifers truly love themselves and their partner. Their Self-Esteem Bucket is full so they have a lot of love to give. Recently, Marie and Dennis came to a roadblock in their relationship. Marie had the opportunity to go to New York on a scholarship to study medicine. She had asked my advice on whether she should go. I told her, "I'm going to miss you terribly, but if it's truly what you want to do, and it sounds like an incredible **opportunity**, then I say go for it!" So how did Dennis respond? Almost exactly the same as I had. He told her he loved her, and wanted the best for her. He put aside his own desires of having her close, and put her needs first. They talked about different options, including his moving down there in a couple of years. The bottom line was, it was Marie's choice, and he didn't try to control her decision. That's a healthy relationship!

After hours of debating, she was ready to go, only to discover that she couldn't accept this scholarship after all because she wasn't a U.S. citizen. But as she told me later, "If one good thing came out of this, I know that Dennis *loves* me enough to encourage me to move towards my dreams, even if that means putting geographical distance between us."

Many Roots

A key blessing to being a Lifer is that you have many roots: friends, family and others who **support** you. A tree with too few roots will not remain standing for long. Similarly, we humans need more than one relationship to sustain us. Since no one is perfect, one person cannot meet all of our needs. Therefore, it is important to have many supportive roots in our life.

But the Disguised want to cut off your roots, because it means you have other people who have influence on you. The Disguised will do this by saying put-downs about your friends or getting angry when you spend time with them. While the Blind will believe these criticisms and cut their

Many lifers will invest into several relationships. Even if they have a relationship partner they will continue to spend their free time with their friends. This is healthy because different friends provide different support.
Also if the relationship ends, the lifer has several people (roots) to rely on.

roots off to salvage their relationship, the Lifers will often see the put-downs as a **red** light, and often end the relationship.

No one person can meet all our needs. As much as you think you've met your Prince Charming, he's not perfect and neither are you. I fully believe we are created as relational people. We need people–but we can't put all our needs onto one person. The Lifers understand this. While they may strongly **PURSUE** their relationships, they still maintain their friendships–and this is so important! Different people provide different support for us. Dating relationships come and go, while friendships hopefully represent stability for us!

Obviously, to maintain friendships you need time. The Lifers give each other space and time. While the Disguised often are jealous when their partner is going out with their friends, the Lifers don't feel jealous or threatened by other friends. They know it is important to have friendships, and they encourage it. All our friends and family are the "roots" that provide us with balance and variety. Especially in times of crisis, we all need many roots. While the Blind and Disguised might say after getting dumped, "My life is over," the Lifer might be upset and sad but know that they have roots they can rely on.

The Head and the Heart

A few years ago I dated this guy Dylan from Florida. I met him while filming for my TV show, and we fell "totally in love." He was an artist, romantic, loving and seemed too good to be true. He flew me to his home to see him for Thanksgiving, and we had an incredible time. A couple of months later, he came to see me in Toronto, in my own environment, and the "red lights" started to appear. I noticed that he had very few positive things to say. I remember taking him with Marie and Dennis to see the loft I had just bought. Walking out of there, he said, "The place is really small. I can't stand the city. It's so noisy. I want to live in the country." By the end of the visit I confronted him. "I feel as though anything that I have to show you, you are critical of. Are you purposely trying to put me down to elevate yourself?" He didn't say anything at first. After a while he responded, "Karyn, you are too put together. For a guy, it's intimidating. I have to admit, it's difficult to encourage you. And yeah, that's probably why I do put you down."

To anybody on the **outside**, it looked like an easy decision–dump him! But when you're on the inside and you feel "totally in love" it's more difficult to make a good decision. A real dilemma! I now have my "head and heart" rule of thumb. I listen to what my head tells me and then what my heart tells me. My heart tells me feelings and some random thoughts that I haven't questioned. My head tells me reality, facts and the **truth**.

Naturally, the messages were very different. My **rule**, which has worked well, is if my head and heart tell me the same message -it's a good decision. But if they are giving conflicting messages-listen to the head! It's more reliable! **If you're having difficulty figuring out what your head is telling you, listen to what your friends and parents are saying.** People outside of your situation are often more objective. Because they're not the ones "in love," their judgement is not clouded. Parents and friends who really care about you will often point out "red lights" so listen to them! The famous saying "Love is blind" is true. When we "fall in love" we often turn our heads off so we're blind to

important head messages. Often when I counsel teens they admit after a break-up that, while with their partner, they saw "red lights" that caused them much grief but ignored or downplayed them. So unlike the Hollywood movies that tell us to, "Follow your heart," I encourage you to "Follow your Head as well as your Heart!" It will help you make wise decisions!

Once I had done this heart/head exercise, I ended the relationship with Dylan. Darlene told me, "Well, Karyn, it took you only 2 months to come to your senses–but it took me 4 1/2 years to make a decision about Luke."

I think it is so important to always learn from our experiences, so that we don't repeat the same mistakes. As long as we learn from our experiences, we are growing as a person. If we don't stop and learn, we often repeat the same pattern. So often we blame others. But I think to be truly a Lifer we need to look and ask ourselves, for example, "What did I learn about myself from dating Dylan?" I learned that I need a Lifer, someone who is truly content with who he is. I learned that I am a romantic and therefore sometimes jump too quickly into relationships. I learned that I need to take more time to truly get to know someone before being committed to them.

Know Their "Sex-Value"

Lifers also know their value on sex. Obviously, when we're talking about relationships and dating, sex is an important topic to discuss! When I counsel teens I'll often ask them, "What is your value for sex?" They usually look at me strangely and say, "What are you talking about?" I'll explain that everyone decides whether sexual activity is of great or little importance to them. Their "value decision" will greatly impact their actions. For example, let's say that three people look at the same car for sale. One person might say, "It's worth $45,000" to me". The second person might say, "No way, only $10,000." The third person would say, "$5000 is all I would pay for it". It's the same car yet there are three different opinions or values for the car. How do you think the third person would treat the car compared to the first? My guess is that the first person would treat their car with utmost care. They would drive safely and be careful with who they would lend their car to. They would take pride in their car and treat it with respect. I'll bet that the third person would be more risky and less cautious. The car isn't worth very much to them, so they are more likely to treat it poorly or abuse it. They don't care who drives it because if it gets damaged, it's not a big deal.

My point is that the more we value something, the more likely we are to take really good care of it. That's why sex and self-esteem are connected. The more I value myself and my body, the more careful I am in deciding what sexual activity I engage in. If I'm a Lifer, I know that I'm important. I know that my body is important. I know my sexual boundaries. I know my limits and how "far I will go". Once I've made my decision I know how to <u>stick to it</u>!

I counselled 17-year old Francis. She had been dating her boyfriend for almost a year and they had not had sex. So I asked her about her value. She responded, "Karyn, I don't really know. I would kind of like to wait till I'm married, but that seems unrealistic. I really love David, but I find myself looking at other guys as well. I just keep thinking that we've been dating for almost a year so it just seems like the next step. David really wants to and I feel bad if I don't give him what he wants. Besides I'm the only one of my friends who has not had sex yet". I stopped her and asked, "Francis, what do YOU want? What is your goal? How would your value change if it was common in North America to wait for sex until marriage? Would you want to wait until you're older? Finished high school? In university? Married?" She paused and said, "Yeah, I think I would want to wait ` till I'm married." A surprised look came over her face. I think she was shocked at her own response. I continued, "It sounds like your value of sex is highly based on our culture and your friends. Because many teens are engaging in sex, you think that is what you should be doing. Let me challenge you to stop and think for yourself. What do you want? If you honestly want to wait until you're married, you need to make a plan to keep this goal. What do you need to do, or not do, to keep this goal. How "far" will you go? What ENVIRONMENTS or places make it more difficult to keep this goal? What do you need to tell your boyfriend? Which friends will discourage you from reaching this goal? Which friends will encourage you towards this goal? Who could help you be accountable for this goal? Make a plan (goal setting steps are discussed in Third Base). And stick to it!"

Abstinence is a tough goal, but realistic and well worth it according to my good friend, Danny. At **28** years old, he lost his virginity to his wife on their wedding day! Although most of his friends and fellow athletes did not share his goal, Danny held his value through high school, university and grad school. This goal was not easy to keep. But he kept focused on his goal. He valued himself and he valued the idea of giving his wife that special part of himself on their wedding night. It was "well worth the wait, I wouldn't change anything" he later shared with me! His wife felt extremely cherished!

Danny's story is the exception in North America today, however, I share this story to let you know it is a **possible** option even in our culture! The important point is to figure out YOUR value and design a plan to keep it! When I ask teens what their value is for sex, here are some common answers I hear:

"I want to wait till I'm in love"
"I'll just know. Whenever it feels right"
"I want to wait until I could handle the possibility of being pregnant"
"Sex is really no big deal. I'm young, I just want it whenever I feel like it"

"I want to wait till I have a serious partner"
"I'm not sure. I've never thought about it"
"I want to wait till I'm eighteen or older"

This is a very **PERSONAL** decision and one worth thinking over. Allow me to just caution you to **think** about this before you get in "a heated moment". As I shared with you earlier, use your **head** <u>and</u> your heart! <u>Think</u> of the big picture. If your value is to "wait till it feels right" or "until I'm in love", you are relying on your feelings, which can be deceiving. Think about this value. How many people do you think you will "fall in love" with between now and when you make a lifetime commitment? Will it bother you if you've slept with five, ten or fifteen people between now and then? How will you feel about yourself? How will your life partner feel? The key is to think **ahead** and not just about today. **CHAL-LENGE** your value. Are you sleeping with your partner to "please" or "keep them"? What are potential risks of your value (ie. relationship ends, pregnancy, acquiring a sexually transmitted disease)? How would you handle these risks if they happened to you? What are the potential rewards of your value? I know this sounds boring and like a speech from a parent, but I speak as a counsellor who works with hundreds of teens who think too late. Remember to stick to <u>what your head and heart tell you!</u>

Just remember that today is a new day, a fresh start. It doesn't matter if you are already sexually active, treat yourself with respect and claim your new value today. There are many teens I've worked with that became sexually active and later regret their decisions. They would often say, "Well I started now, I might as well have sex with my other partners. They know I'm not a virgin and they will expect it." Remember, we learn from our past choices. It doesn't matter what you did before, claim your new value. Find an **accountability** partner to help you keep your goal. Make a plan of how you are going to keep your value. Remember that you are valuable and deserve to be treated with respect! Learn to say yes to what you want and no to what you don't want. Your body **BELONGS** to you, not your partners. If your partner really cares about you, they will respect your boundaries and will not try to convince you to change your value!

SECOND BASE: The Impact

How does your attitude about yourself affect your communication style?

COMMUNICATION STYLE:
The Blind may
* be passive-aggressive and **AVOID** conflict
* when upset or angry with someone, tell a third person and avoid telling the first person directly how they feel
* "back stab" other people
* use **"she"** or "he" statements (e.g., "She makes me so angry.")
* **lack** confidence to stand up for their own opinions or thoughts
* flip between avoiding and attacking

When I was **17** years old, one of my good friends was Britney, a girl from my high school who was outgoing and popular. I remember feeling privileged that Britney took the time to get to know me. However, I noticed that she back stabbed many of our friends. She would compliment them to their face, but once they were out of sight, the insults would start flowing from her.

Although Britney appeared confident she **lacked** confidence to talk with our friends directly about things that concerned or bothered her. So she chose to avoid them and verbally attack them, criticising them to other people.

Someone once told me, "If people back stab others, they're back stabbing you, too!" But I thought there was no way Britney would ever do that to me. I was wrong, and I **learned** the hard way.

Instead of addressing conflicts with people directly, Britney would "vent" about them with other people. This is called passive-aggressive behaviour, and it causes two main problems: First, it creates a feeling of distrust, which builds walls in friendships. Many people will pull back from friendships if they don't feel they can trust someone. Second, avoiding or being passive-aggressive doesn't solve any problems. Venting your frustration to a third party only gets more people involved and adds *chaos* to the situation. When people are telling third parties, it is often because they want to get people on their side, as if to start a minor war. The need to get people on your side is another sign of insecurity.

COMMUNICATION STYLE:
The Disguised may
* be aggressive and attack others verbally
* feel their opinion is more important than others' opinions
* act **arrogant** to force their opinion

* firmly, sometimes rudely, stand up for their opinion
* sound **angry** when they talk
* lack respect for others' opinions and cut people off
* make "You" (derogatory) statements (e.g., "You are so stupid.")
* cause tension and distance in relationships (with friends, in dating relationships and with parents)

In my first year of counselling, **15**-year-old Stephen was sent to see me to deal with his "communication problems." His parents had had enough! Apparently he was rude, arrogant and frequently told them where to go. When he communicated, he didn't care how it came out or how it made the receiver feel. He would make statements such as "I hate you," "You're the worst parents," "You're so unfair," "I want to have any parents other than you." His communication sounded like verbal weapons. How he talked translated to "Life is unfair so I'm going to **HURT** you to build myself up."

When Stephen came to see me, I saw a different side. He was bitter, angry, frustrated and very sad. He had gone through many trials in his life, including physical abuse and abandonment by his father, adjusting to a stepfather, and coping with a learning disability. His strong feelings had never been talked about or dealt with. They were buried. The more I talked with Stephen, the more I realised that he felt **abandoned** and angry at the world. This anger came out in his communication style.

Deep down, Stephen was Disguised in his communication style. He built himself up by putting people down. This style had many consequences. First, it caused real tension between him and his parents. The tension was so great that he moved out at 15 years old, and lived on the streets for almost a year. His girlfriend, who was Blind, took the aggressive comments and unfortunately believed them. As a result, her self-esteem deteriorated. While some of his friends would "take" the aggressive comments, many would not, which resulted in friends abandoning him. Naturally, his friends leaving him brought back the same feelings as when his father abandoned him, which made him even more angry and *bitter*. Overall, Stephen alienated himself from his family and friends because of his communication style. Did he see this? No! In fact, he continually told me, "Karyn, I haven't done anything wrong. It's all their fault." Unfortunately I was able to work with Stephen for only a short time before he was kicked out of his home. I never saw him again.

COMMUNICATION STYLE:
The Lifers often

* are truth-tellers and **ASSERTIVE**
* feel their opinions and thoughts are important
* feel confident enough to share their thoughts with others
* firmly stand up for their opinions and feelings
* **RESPECT** other people's viewpoint
* use "I" statements (e.g., "I feel frustrated when... .")

One of the main goals Stephen and I worked on was for him to be less aggressive and more assertive. He frequently told his parents he hated them. Was it true? No. He just used this as a verbal weapon to get their attention. I challenged him to tell them the truth–not for them, but for him. What was the truth? He was frustrated that they expected a B average even with his learning disability, and he felt that they didn't treat him with respect.

I challenged Stephen to be the mature one and start being assertive–start telling the truth. We designed a plan. Stephen had just got his report card and when his stepdad saw the Cs he freaked on him, saying accusingly, "You didn't study, and you're not going to amount to anything." Stephen would have verbally attacked him back, in his old aggressive style. But with a few counselling hours behind him, he turned to his stepdad and said, "Gary, I'm frustrated when you say I'm not going to amount to anything. I tried my best–and C's are all I can do." His stepdad was caught off **guard**. He couldn't believe that Stephen didn't lose it in an outburst. Gary still responded, "Well I think you could have tried harder." Stephen told me that being assertive didn't cure the tension between him and his stepdad, but the arguments and tensions were greatly **REDUCED**!

The key to being assertive is to use "I" statements. For example, Stephen focussed on how he felt by saying, "I feel . . . ." Being assertive has so many advantages. First, your audience will listen. If someone said to me, "Karyn, you are so frustrating," instantly I would get defensive and tune out. However, if someone said, "I **FEEL** frustrated, Karyn, when you do this . . .," then I would be open to what they had to say. Since people are usually more willing to listen to an **"I"** statement, there is a better chance that the problem will be resolved.

Second, being assertive builds our self-esteem, because we are validating our feelings and our opinions. Sonja, a 19-year-old teen, and I worked together for months on being more assertive. One day she told me, "I've learned to be assertive with my boyfriend and I love it. He has more respect for me because I'm **sticking** up for my opinions. And I feel great about myself. I never thought I could do it!"

Remember that being assertive is for yourself-not in hopes of changing the other person. Many times when I challenge teens to be assertive with their parents or friends they say, "No, it's not going to change them." If your motive for being assertive is to change them, you will probably be disappointed. But if your goal is to stick up for your opinion, then even if they respond the same way, it's a victory for you! Finally, when you're **assertive**, you deal with the situation head-on. It's a done deal-no anger or bitterness builds up.

I realised this when I was 18 years old. At that time, I faced the choice of being assertive or not. My boyfriend, Stuart, was house-sitting his parents' friend Bill's gorgeous home, including its pool and hot tub, for one week. On the Saturday, we decided to hang out there. We had a great day swimming, and hanging out in the pool. No, we were not making out! Well, the next-door neighbour, a nosy man, kept staring at the two of us in the hot tub. I never thought anything of it. The following week, Bill was over at Stuart's house, jokingly telling his parents, "My neighbour told me that Karyn and Stuart had a heated moment in my hot tub. He said he couldn't take his eyes off Karyn. But my neighbour literally died of a heart attack the next day. I think seeing Karyn was too much for him. It killed my neighbour!"

When I heard this, I felt extremely *irritated.* First, we were not making out in the hot tub. Second, his neighbour really did have a heart attack, and I didn't think that we should be joking about it. But I pretended that it didn't really bother me.

However, the following week, Stuart and I went to a party, and six people shared with us the "news" that they'd heard we were having sex in the hot tub. Apparently Bill had told a few people, and the story, like runaway gossip, kept getting worse.

I was so angry! If the story were true, I would be embarrassed. But it wasn't even remotely true! And I was angry with Bill, our so-called "friend", for going around spreading these **rumours**. That night, after the party, I called Bill up and told him we needed to talk. Stuart thought I was crazy; he would have preferred to forget and avoid the whole situation. But there was no way I would do that.

So at 3:00 a.m., Bill came over to Stuart's house and we talked about it. I told him how frustrated and embarrassed I was. I focussed on my feelings rather than attacking him, since I knew that would be more productive. Since Bill was a family friend, he was receptive to what we discussed and agreed to talk the next day to the people he'd told the rumour to and speak the truth!

It felt so good to **CONFRONT** the situation, and once I had, it was a done deal. We could move on. I didn't harbour anger or bitter feelings towards Bill. If anything, it was the opposite. I gained respect for him from the manner in which he handled the situation.

It's important to remember that we cannot control other people. But we can control how we respond to others. I couldn't control what Bill was saying, but I could control how I responded to Bill. By focussing on what I can control, being proactive, I felt empowered and better about myself.

SECOND BASE: The Impact

How does your attitude about yourself affect how you set goals?

SETTING GOALS:

The Blind may

* set very high, unrealistic goals, often setting themselves up for disappointment
* often see obstacles as crisis situations
* be **PERFECTIONIST**, striving to be perfect, with unrealistic goals and therefore they are seldom content
* procrastinate tasks because they are striving to be "perfect," and since nothing is ever perfect enough, they keep putting their tasks off
* set low goals or **avoid** setting goals altogether for fear of failure[vii]
* avoid trying new things

I will never forget coming out of a science exam with my "perfect" friend Stephanie. I thought I had done O.K, but Stephanie was practically crying. She thought she had failed. She'd never failed an exam in her life. Two weeks later, when we received the marks, she'd got 84%, and I'd got 67%. She looked devastated! She'd hoped for a 90% and had fallen short of her goal. It seemed that whatever mark or goal Stephanie strived for, she was never satisfied. Meanwhile, I was just happy I'd passed.

I noticed that Stephanie was also a **PROCRASTI-NATOR.** Because she aimed to do tasks "perfectly," which is impossible, she would procrastinate, and put things off because she knew they could never be perfect. Sometimes, projects would be 90% finished, and she wouldn't hand them in because she knew they weren't perfect.

Stephanie was striving for external self-esteem, based on things outside herself. She would tell herself messages such as, "If I get 90%, I'm OK." This is conditional self-esteem. Her self-esteem was dependent on her receiving high marks. So, naturally, she set high goals for herself to prove that she was lovable. The problem was that if she tried her **ABSOLUTE** best and got a 75%, she would be depressed and mad at herself. That is so unfair – we shouldn't be mad at ourselves when we try our best because many things are out of our control and may prevent us from reaching our goal (e.g., a tough exam or a tough marker). It's great to set goals, and sometimes even high goals, but Stephanie's goal was not to "try her best." Her goal was to "get 90%, no matter what." As a result, she was tough on herself.

Setting high, unrealistic goals is common for the Blind. It's almost as if they purposely set themselves up for disappointment. They strive for these goals, which seem unrealistic and nearly impossible to achieve.

A guy I counselled, Markus, was exactly the opposite. He rarely set any goals. He lived his life day-to-day. His only goal or mission in life was to "never worry and never plan ahead, because that could lead to worry and disappointment." He didn't ask any girls out, and **REFUSED** to try out for any sports. He also refused to find a part-time job, while complaining that he had no money. On the outside, he might have looked lazy. But on the inside, I think he was afraid of rejection or failure.

Stephanie and Markus seemed different outwardly, but **internally**, they were both Blind. Neither was happy about themself. Both complained about their weaknesses and were Blind to their strengths. Perhaps knowingly or unknowingly, they both set themselves up for hardship. Stephanie set herself up for disappointment by setting unrealistic goals. Markus avoided rejection by not setting any goals. Neither realised how their actions were affecting their self-esteem.

SETTING GOALS:
Similar to the Blind, the Disguised may

* set very high, unrealistic goals, often setting themselves up for disappointment
* often see obstacles as crisis situations
* be perfectionists, striving to be perfect, with unrealistic goals–therefore seldom content
* procrastinate tasks because they're striving to be "perfect"
* set very few goals, not wanting to risk failure
* avoid change or trying new things, for fear of failure

Yet, they also may

* set very high or **daredevil** goals, to show off and/or put others down
* have no fear about dying or may think, "Who cares if I die doing this stunt? I want to prove to myself and my friends that I am better than they are."
* think only about day-to-day or short-term goals (e.g., What am I doing tonight?)
* view setting long-term goals as "a waste of time," "useless," or "boring." (In reality, setting a long-term goal means having an expectation, which might lead to disappointment.)

For an entire year I counselled Jack, a 13-year-old who had severe anger and aggressive behaviour. Since setting goals is a large part of counselling, I asked him what he wanted to work on or improve about himself during our counselling time together. He said, "Nothing. I'm perfect." So I talked about what was important to him and avoided using the word "goals." He shared his love for skateboarding on rooftops and jumping off high buildings. When I asked him if he was afraid, he said, "No way. Who cares if I die? At least I would die doing something I love." Yet as we talked about his daredevil stunts, I discovered he did them only when his "friends" were around. Jack admitted that there was a lot of pressure to "beat the last guy's move." Jack was basing his attitude about himself on **externals**. If he beat the last guy's move, he would feel accepted. He built himself up by putting others down.

What I found most surprising was his "No Fear" attitude. He didn't care if he lived or died. His skateboarding and jumping from rooftops were so important to him he would die for them. After I worked with Jack for months, he finally admitted that he felt empty inside. He had no joy, no love for life. His only pleasure was to prove to his friends that he was acceptable by beating their skateboarding moves. He was focussing on externals and conditions to feel good about himself instead of looking within himself. He hated the word "goals" because to him it represented **"expectations"** and "what my parents want."

SETTING GOALS:
The Lifers often
* are more likely to have higher career goals[viii]
* are more likely to be motivated and strive for excellence[ix]

* believe in themselves, which helps them do well
* set **REALISTIC** goals and attain them
* plan small steps towards their realistic goals
* see crises as opportunities to be seized, or challenges to be met
* set external goals (e.g., trying out for a sport) and internal goals (e.g., aiming to be a kinder person)
* set goals and improvements for themselves without comparing themselves to others
* know what they want and set their own goals (not what their parents or friends want)
* have **confidence** in their goal setting
* like trying new things
* aim to try their best
* evaluate their progress as they move towards their goals
* are not afraid of failing, as long as they've tried their best
* set short-term and long-term goals
* are not afraid to make a mistake
* **LEARN** from past mistakes

When I was in Grade 9, I faced a crisis when I received my very first exam back. I'd got **38%**. I wish I could say that I hadn't studied, thereby explaining the low mark. But, in reality, I had studied for this English exam, which made it very frustrating. In Grade 8, I had completed several learning style tests. It had been discovered that I had some kind of learning disability. In Grade 9, after receiving this exam back, I was devastated. I clearly remember walking home, with this 38% exam in my hand, bawling my eyes out. I thought to myself, "Your life is worthless. You'll never finish high school, and you'd better forget university." I was angry with myself. Good grades were important to me. Meanwhile, some of my closest friends got As and Bs with barely studying.

That walk home was a pivotal point in my life. I remember feeling so **devastated** and alone. And yet in the midst of it, I recognised something: "Wait a second, I have a choice. I can either give up and do nothing with my life, or I can give it my absolute best."

That night, I thought up my plan. I was going to go in for extra help from my teacher (which I had always avoided), and get a tutor. This "crisis" was now an obstacle, and I had a choice of two directions I could take. Either my life would be a waste, or I was going to do everything in my power to overcome it. My average was 62%, and my goal was to get to 68% by the end of Grade 9. I achieved my goal!

At first, when I got my 68%, I was proud of myself for working diligently and achieving my goal. That is, until my close friend, Loreli, someone who rarely studied, got 84%. I started feeling frustrated again. Then I realised this was a self-defeating pattern in me. I would set a goal, get it and feel good about myself, until I started **comparing** myself to others. But that day I made a pact with myself not to compare myself to anyone else. It's great to look at others for motivation, but if it's going to pull a person down and make them feel inadequate–it's not worth it. So I focussed on comparing my actual average to my goal average, and not to anyone else's average.

When we set goals and achieve them, it's the most incredible feeling! Sure it was great to watch my school average rise, but as I look back, the rise in marks was the secondary reward. The most important lesson I learned was that I could have an impact on my life! Instead of my life just "happening to me," I could actually make a difference in how my life was going to unfold. It's like my life was a book, and instead of reading and waiting to see how it was going to end, I could write my own chapters. For the first time, I realised that life is nothing but a series of thousands of choices and decisions. My learning disability was a circumstance that I couldn't control without help. But I could control how I reacted to that "crisis." Was it an obstacle that would stop me from pursuing my dreams? Or was it merely a challenge that I had to figure out how to meet?

I can honestly say that having that learning disability was one of the best things that ever happened to me. I felt I was forced to choose between perceiving it as an "obstacle" or as a "challenge." Overcoming that "challenge" took a lot of PERSEVERANCE, planning and prayer. But without realising it, I slowly began building internal self-esteem. I was going to take action for the events in my life, not passively watch everything unfold! After the school goals, I started setting goals in every other part of my life: socially, travelling, part-time job, money, relationships, etc. Setting goals is to me a crucial aspect of my personal and business life. The goals lay out the path and direction that I aim to travel.

Think of goals as being like a map. If I were to plan a trip to Europe and just show up in some country and begin touring, my trip might be quite chaotic. I might end up going in circles, having difficulty speaking the language, and learn that I need certain visas for some countries. But if I plan out my trip, figure out where I want to go, how many days I have, then I have direction and guidance. It doesn't mean that I can't change my plan, but at least I have some structure of where I want to go and how I'm going to get there. I'll spend more time seeing the sights and less time going in circles. Goal setting is similar. It maps out where you want to go and what is important to you. You can always make changes along the way, but at least you have some structure of what you want to do and who you want to become in your life. The best part of setting goals is that it is very **EMPOWERING**. Just think, Who is the person you want to become? What are your goals in regards to school, friends, parents, career, part-time job, money, travelling? Let yourself dream!

SECOND BASE: The Impact
How does your attitude about yourself influence self-destructive behaviours?

SELF-DESTRUCTIVE BEHAVIOUR:
The Blind & Disguised

* may self-mutilate (physically punishing themselves through scratching, cutting, severe piercing) to forget about their pain
* may under-eat or overeat to feel in control of their life
* may use drugs to "make them feel better" and "help them forget problems such as depression"[xi]
* are more likely to **abuse alcohol**[xii]
* are more likely to seek and accept negative feedback[xiii]
* are more likely to abuse drugs[xiv]
* are more likely to have an eating disorder (girls)[xv]
* are more likely to smoke (girls)[xvi]

STATISTICS

* self-injury is 10 times more popular than suicide for youth[xvii]
* 54% of teens will have tried an illegal drug by the end of high school[xviii]
* the most popular illegal drugs are marijuana followed by ecstasy, steroids and heroin[xix]

Self-Mutilation

Two years ago, I spoke at a high school of 500 students tucked away in a tiny community in Northern Ontario. The principal had asked me to arrive early to discuss some "problems" that many of his students had. As soon as I arrived, he took me to a room where there were 12 others, teachers, counsellors, and parents. They were very **scared** and worried about their students. One parent began talking and crying a little: "Karyn, I'm afraid. My daughter is mutilating herself. Her arms are all cut up. Why is she doing this, and how can we help her?" I told this group that I would address the subject in my self-esteem presentation.

I talked about how when some people feel down about themselves, they do things to help them forget about their problems. Their actions may include self-mutilation. I believe people mutilate for different reasons. For some, they have seen it done on music videos. Others do it because their friends are doing it. Many hurt themselves when they strive for a goal and don't get it. The most common statement I hear from teens that mutilate themselves is, "Karyn, I would rather feel physical pain than the **emotional** hurt that I have in my life." Overall, they feel angry, sad, hurt and frustrated about some part of their life. Instead of talking about it, they harm themselves.

I shared the following true story with that high school audience: "I counselled a girl named Jackie who was addicted to cutting herself. She would set a goal for herself and if she didn't attain it, she would take a razor to her arm. It was her way of punishing herself. It didn't matter if her goal was too high or she'd tried her best. If it wasn't reached, the punishment would follow."

After the high school workshop, I saw out of the corner of my eye this one girl walking towards me. She was **CRYING** so hard that she was heaving. She told me, "Karyn, you are the first person who's explained to me why I am doing this." I asked her, "Doing what?" She didn't answer but held her arm up and pulled up her sleeve, showing me her arm. I can't even explain in words what I saw. But it looked like a dog had chewed up her arm. It was completely cut up and scarred. She shared with me that when she felt upset or mad, she would hurt herself. It was her way of **"escaping"** her pain. She admitted that her emotional pain was so deep inside, she would rather feel physical pain. Cutting herself took her mind off her "problems." But it wasn't until she heard me speak that she realised self-mutilation was connected to low self-esteem. She just did it because, as she said, "It makes me forget about my problems for a little bit."

Think about it. It makes sense. The Blind hurt themselves with verbal statements such as, "You're worthless," or "You're not going to amount to anything." And now we know that some attack themselves physically as well. This girl, who was **addicted** to mutilating herself, decided that day to stop her habit. She made the goal that when she was angry or upset she would talk to her best friend. I also got her set up with one of the guidance counsellors at her school.

I ended up seeing this girl 3 weeks later and couldn't believe the **difference**! I was leading a follow-up workshop with a smaller group of students. And this girl openly shared with the group her former habit. She had stopped cutting herself cold turkey and was like a different person–smiling and beaming! She still had a lot of hurt that she was trying to sort out, but at least she wasn't punishing herself in the process.

Under-eating & Overeating

Another "escape" is under-eating or overeating. I remember in university, after we received our exams back, my friends and I headed down to the cafeteria. I grabbed my lunch and waited for my friend Lorraine. I asked her where her lunch was and she responded, "I'm not going to eat today. I don't deserve it. I got only 84% in math, and my goal was 85%." She set herself a goal, and since she didn't attain it, she punished herself. Lorraine didn't care that she'd tried her **BEST** and that the exam was hard. She only focussed on her lack of attaining her goal! Lorraine's self-esteem was based on the externals: "If I get a good mark, I'll be happy with myself. If I don't, I will hurt myself."

The opposite extreme to Lorraine's problem is overeating. I counselled a woman named Paula. While Lorraine would stop eating when she was **upset**, Paula would eat when she was troubled. Food didn't represent nourishment for her body–it represented an escape. When Paula ate, she would forget about her problems and feel in control. Since she had many problems, she ate often, and as a result became quite obese, in an effort to feel more powerful. This started a pattern. Paula would be upset, eat, gain weight, then feel worse, and as a result would eat more. Instead of dealing with her feelings directly, she would passively deal with them by eating to forget her problems. Food was a Quick Fix. At the moment, she would feel better when she ate. But minutes or hours later, she would feel out-of-control and want to lose the weight.

Drugs

Another escape that I hear of from many parents is the use of drugs. As I've said before, it's so easy to look at the exterior problem, "My daughter is using cocaine." But that's not really the problem—that's only what we see, the symptom. There is something much stronger happening underneath. When I counsel teens, I try to uncover a person's basic motives. I counselled Trevor, a **17**-year-old who frequently used pot and mushrooms, and occasionally acid. It was interesting to listen to his sales pitch, trying to convince me that using drugs is OK. While it concerned me that he used them, I realised it was his choice. But I was even more interested as to why he used them. What was his motivation? What happened when he used a drug? How did he feel? He said that the drugs increased his creativity, allowed helped him to relax, helped him not to care about what other people thought of him, enabled him to forget about his problems, and, overall, made him feel better about himself.

There was his motive. He admitted it himself. Taking drugs was his way of "feeling better"–a Quick Fix, an external way to increase his self-esteem and to escape from unwanted feelings. He said that he had learned to be "himself" while using drugs. I challenged him, saying that he could only truly be himself without the drugs.

SELF-DESTRUCTIVE BEHAVIOUR:
The Lifers

* do not self-mutilate (they like themselves and don't want to hurt themselves)
* set **realistic** goals, which they often attain, and there fore feel in control of their life, which eliminates thoughts of under-eating or overeating
* are less likely to misuse alcohol[xx]
* are more likely to seek and **ACCEPT** positive feedback from others[xxi]
* are more likely not to smoke[xxii]
* are more likely to be satisfied with their body image[xxiii]

This section is short, because the Lifers would **not** think of hurting themselves. If they set a goal and didn't attain it, the Lifers would analyse that goal pattern. Did they try their best? If so, they would be disappointed, but then let it go. If they didn't try their best, they might be mad at themselves, learn from their mistake and **MOVE** on. But self-inflicted punishment would not be an option.

I have worked with many Blind and Disguised teens who mutilate themselves. And almost every time, the first goal that they set in counselling is to stop hurting themselves, physically and emotionally!

With respect to eating, many people think a diet has something to do with food and weight loss. Sometimes it does, but many times it doesn't. Of the many teens I've worked with who are anorexic or bulimic, although they complain about "being too fat," most are already slim. It doesn't make any sense, does it? But their addiction to food, or lack of it, is usually more about control. Often these teens have lost some control in their life: the parents divorce, the boyfriend dumps them, they lack money, they are dealing with abuse, they have social difficulties, they get poor grades, etc. It is an awful feeling to be "out of control," so our mind finds something it can control, our body! When my friend Lorraine didn't get the mark she wanted, she felt "out of control," and tried to regain control of her body by not eating that day.

There are some Lifers who may overeat or under-eat; however, I like to focus on one's motive. Some Lifers who appear to overeat may just like food, enjoy eating out, find exercise boring, or have a low metabolism and therefore gain weight. Some Lifers who appear to under-eat may be picky eaters, or have a high metabolism and therefore put on very little weight. So once again it comes back to motive. Is the person trying to gain weight or lose weight? Are they being careless in regards to their health? Are there medical issues beyond their control? The key difference between the Lifers who under-eat/overeat and Disguised and Blind who under-eat/overeat is their **motive**. The Lifers do not aim to hurt themselves while the Disguised and Blind want to feel in control and may abuse or hurt their body, or someone else.

Drugs . . . what a big topic! My focus as a counsellor, once again, is to look at the motivation! Be honest with yourself. If you use drugs, what is your motive? Why do you use them? Is it peer pressure? Do you want to "escape" for a while? Are you curious? Do they increase your creativity? Do you feel better about yourself? Are you more outgoing? Are you addicted?

I don't want to generalise by saying that the Blind and Disguised all use drugs. That is definitely not true. Nor am I saying that Lifers don't use or experiment with drugs. But I can say that the Blind and Disguised are more **vulnerable** to trying drugs. Remember, they want to fit in, they don't feel comfortable about themselves, and they often will do things externally to build themselves up. They may use drugs to "fill their self-esteem bucket."

What is an **ADDICTION**? An addiction can be a craving for anything or anybody–drugs, shopping, sex, the Internet, another person (girlfriend/boyfriend)–that you feel you need and can't be without. If you think you're not addicted to something, try stopping for a week or two. Can you do it? If not, you may be fooling yourself, and in reality you may be addicted.

SECOND BASE: The Impact
How does your attitude about yourself affect depression and suicide?

DEPRESSION AND SUICIDE:
The Blind & Disguised

* are more likely to be depressed, hopeless and suicidal[xxiv]

* who are feeling depressed, may lose motivation, sleep too much or not enough, have difficulty concentrating, feel worthless, have difficulty making decisions, have less energy, have a loss of appetite, have thoughts of death or plan their suicide[xxv]

* may withdraw from their friends, prefer to be isolated or alone, or lose interest in their hobbies

93

* may often look for **negative** friends, music or environments that confirm how they are already feeling about themselves[xxvi]
* may use drugs or alcohol to numb their feelings of depression and help them escape[xxvii]

STATISTICS

* Suicide is the second leading cause of death for youth in Canada after motor vehicle accidents.[xxviii]
* Suicide is the third leading cause of death for youth in the U.S. after motor vehicle accidents and unintentional injury[xxix]
* Suicide has tripled from 1952 to 1992 among teens in the U.S.[xxx]
* In Australia, 25% of all male deaths and 17% of female deaths in 1995 were from suicide.[xxxi]
* In Canada, 2.7% of youth 12-14 years old are at risk for depression, compared to 9.2% of youth 15-19 years old.[xxxii]
* In Canada, of youth 15-19 years old, females are twice as likely as males to be depressed.[xxxiii]

Depression and suicide are a **SCARY** part of our youth culture today. Suicide, a preventable act, is the second highest cause of death for youth in Canada,[xxxiv] and the third highest in the U.S.A.[xxxv] Can you imagine if someone said, "We've found the cure for cancer. It can now be prevented"? There would be thousands of people celebrating! Yet, suicide (often the result of a long depression) is a form of death that is totally preventable!

In my experience, depression is definitely the most common "problem" that I hear of from the youth around me. Many times I'll get a call from a concerned parent saying, "I think my son is depressed, and I don't know what to do." Sometimes I feel like saying, "If you feel helpless, you can **IMAGINE** how he's feeling."

Feeling depressed is normal and part of being a human. I think all humans, at times, feel sad and "down." However, when these feelings start controlling your life (e.g., by a decrease in sleeping, problem eating, lack of motivation, keeping you from some of your favourite hobbies, suicidal thoughts), it is definitely time to take a closer look.

Research has shown that people who have low or false self-esteem are more likely to feel depressed, but this **does not mean that all depressed people are Blind or Disguised.** There are some people who have a chemical imbalance in their brain that changes their moods.[xxxvi] For them, depression is a frustrating disease that they learn to cope with through medication and/or counselling.

If you could relate to two or more symptoms listed at the beginning of this section, I highly RECOMMEND that you talk with your doctor, who can refer you to a good counsellor! Your doctor can address your physical needs, and a counsellor can help you with your emotional needs! Find a counsellor with whom you feel comfortable! Search around if you have to, but definitely go to someone who has been recommended!

When I work with teens, I let their doctor deal with the physical side, and I focus on the emotional issues, teaching "tools" for dealing with the depressed feelings so that the feelings no longer control their life. Research has shown that counselling can be as useful as antidepressant medication.[xxxvii]

I describe depression as "being **stuck**." I picture someone who is "stuck" in a pit of mud–they're trying to move forward, but they don't know how and often feel frustrated and helpless.

Trevor, 17 years old, was one youth I counselled for depression. He had been depressed for 4 months before I saw him. He had lost his motivation for going to school, was smoking pot regularly, had severe insomnia, withdrew from friends, wrote poetry focussing on death, and drew artwork about death. His feelings of depression were so intense that at one point he seriously thought about suicide.

I spent months working with Trevor to understand the reasons for his depression. He shared with me the story of the painful break-up with his girlfriend, Sherri. But he quickly added, "I don't care anymore. I'm over it now. My depression doesn't have anything to do with her." Yet anytime I tried to bring it up, he quickly **CHANGED** the topic. I learned from Trevor that he didn't like talking about anything painful. He avoided it, quickly changed the topic or minimised the situation by saying, "It wasn't a big deal." He was not allowing himself to feel pain or hurt–so he buried it. These very strong feelings were buried inside of him, and eventually turned into a depression.

The fact that he got dumped was extremely painful for Trevor. Many of us will be dumped at some point in our life, and it is never pleasant! But for some, it's much more painful than for others. Since Trevor was Blind, his happiness was built on his relationship. He believed, "If I date Sherri, then I'll be happy." The **flip** side is thinking, "If I don't date her, I'll be unhappy." His plan worked as long as he dated Sherri, but as soon as he was dumped, he was unhappy. Obviously, anyone who is dumped will be unhappy. But it depends on how the person views themselves afterwards. Trevor thought he was lovable while dating Sherri, but once she let him go, he felt unlovable. His feelings for himself were completely controlled by Sherri. Trevor was dependent on his girlfriend, which led to rejection and strong sad feelings, which were buried and eventually led to a depression.

Another aspect of Trevor that I noticed was that he was a **PERFECTIONIST**. Everything that he did had to "be perfect." Striving for perfection was an unrealistic goal, another attribute of choosing to be Blind. He would work on a school assignment, almost complete it, find a mistake, and then not hand it in since it wasn't perfect. As a result, he would get an F, for incomplete, and "feel depressed." His goals were unrealistic and so he was setting himself up for disappointment.

If feelings of depression or sadness are not dealt with but kept within ourselves, this often will lead to depression. It is so important to get feelings out—whether it is through talking, writing poetry, doing artwork or whatever activity that allows you to express yourself.

I find that feeling depressed and feeling helpless go hand-in-hand. When we are depressed, we usually feel hopeless or out of control. Dealing with these feelings is addressed in Third Base.

DEPRESSION AND SUICIDE:
The Lifers

* may sometimes feel depressed, but rarely do these feelings control them
* try to be assertive to others with their thoughts and feelings

* try to **FOCUS** on their strengths
* work on or accept their weaknesses
* are more likely to be satisfied with life,[xxxviii] and therefore suicide would not be an option

Depression often has a negative connotation to it, similar to anger. I used to think that feeling angry was a bad thing. We always have a right to our feelings, because we cannot control our feelings. Yet as I will mention in the anger section, anger is a feeling, a sign that something is going on inside of us. **No** one can make you angry. You react to a situation with an irrational thought, your anger trigger is pulled, and angry feelings take over inside you. The result can be a sudden surge of retaliation—an action that might be impulsive and/or harmful to yourself or others. Self-control with rational thoughts and feelings is learned with practice, to cope with irritating situations. It is important to know what triggers your anger. You must also become aware of how you deal with it. Feeling depressed is similar. We all have the right to feel depressed—and there is nothing wrong with that. The question is, How do we deal with it? There is a difference between feeling depressed and being in a depression.

When Trevor was dumped by his girlfriend he felt depressed. Most of us, like Trevor, would also feel depressed and sad in such circumstances. But those depressed feelings turned into a depression. A depression is the sense that the depressed feelings have taken control over your life and will contaminate other parts of your life. For Trevor, this meant that he lost his zest for life, he withdrew from his friends, and smoked pot to help him forget about his feelings. This made him feel even more depressed.

If Trevor were a Lifer, how would he have handled it **DIFFERENTLY**? He would have been sad and depressed about the break-up. But his happiness would not be totally dependent on his girlfriend. He may want to be with her, but he wouldn't need to be with her. As a result, he wouldn't have taken the break-up so personally. Trevor probably would have had other areas of his life that also gave him satisfaction and stability to get over the emotional loss. If he were a Lifer, he probably would have been assertive (see communication section) about his feelings, perhaps talking out his feelings and disappointments to a close friend. Those negative feelings have to get out. If they don't, they linger inside us and inevitably turn into something more harmful.

Dear Karyn,

Last week I read an article in the newspaper about a 14-year old boy in B.C. who killed himself. He was constantly teased at school and was really miserable, miserable enough to end his life. This made me so, so sad. Maybe you could do a show to raise awareness about this sort of thing...

Meagan and Sarah

Dear Meagan and Sarah,

I agree with you that suicide and bullying are huge topics that need to be discussed. Right now, suicide is the second highest killer of teenagers in Canada and the third highest killer of teenagers in the United

States! How tragic that we sometimes become our own worst enemy!

I've counselled many victims of bullies as well as bullies themselves, and I've realised that they are both hurting people! The bullies often appear extremely confident, arrogant and together-yet inside they are falling apart! They mask their own hurt by anger and vent it out on other people. They build themselves up by putting other people down, typically known as producing false self-esteem. Unfortunately, they often prey on those who already seem insecure or suffer from low self-esteem. Those with low self-esteem believe the insults and feel worse, sometimes to the point of suicide. It's a vicious circle!

To Those Being Teased

What are your options? Don't say none - that's a victim response! You have many choices for handling this. You could avoid the bully or bullies, change environments or schools, or tell a teacher or adult whom you trust and who can help you discuss your options. If the teasing is happening on school property or time, school personnel are responsible for your safety-so it's a good idea to get them involved.

Make **your** safety a priority! Avoid keeping silent-because that's when the bully has control over you. Speak to someone you trust. And, most importantly, don't believe the insults. We can choose what to believe! I know that's easier said than done. But bullies often utter absolute lies, and they win if you believe them. You can't control the bully-but you can control what you believe and how you respond.

Focus on building your own self-esteem. Acknowledge your strengths-we all have some! Work on areas about yourself that you're not happy with. The more confident you are, the less you'll believe the insults, and the less you'll be a target for bullies. Focus on yourself and your response to the bully-this you do have control over! Suicide is not the answer. It's a permanent solution to a temporary problem!

To Bullies & Teasers

What's your motive? Be honest with yourself: Why are you doing it, really? Don't say, It's fun or I'm bored-there is a deeper meaning to your actions that needs to be looked at! You're spending time, energy and breath each time a negative comment comes out of your mouth-so what's your motivation?

Do you feel powerful when you're being a bully? In control? The centre of attention? I've learned through counselling teen bullies that many were once bullied themselves or saw bullying modelled in their homes. They once felt out of control and weak so now it's payback time. They hunt down people who are smaller, weaker or younger than themselves whom they think they can control. This solution is a quick fix-a Band-Aid to the problem that can have many consequences. Instead of dealing with their own pain, they temporarily inflict it on someone else! But in reality, the pain is still there, just masked!

Bullying Is a Sign of Weakness, Not Strength

Bullying means someone has not dealt with their own hurt. So start admitting your own feelings-hurt, frustration, anger or lack of control. Talk with someone you trust! When you do, you'll soon realise that your need or desire to tease others is decreasing.

Teasing can be a habit. Think about how you want to change your habit. Know the consequences if you continue and the rewards if you stop. I guarantee you will feel better about yourself if you stop.

Sincerely,
Karyn[xxxix]

Published in the national Canadian magazine *What*, June 2000.

SECOND BASE: The Impact
How does your attitude about yourself affect how you deal with anger?

DEALING WITH ANGER:
The Blind may

* be passive aggressive about their anger ("She made me so angry")
* BOTTLE up their thoughts and feelings by keeping them to themselves
* back stab the person who "made them" feel angry
* blame themselves for feeling anger
* avoid the person they think "made them" feel angry
* feel "numb" by not feeling anything at all
* "explode" over small situations (e.g., road rage, freaking out at parents)

DEALING WITH ANGER:
The Disguised may

* be aggressive and accusating about their anger ("You make me so angry.")
* verbally attack the person they think "made them" feel angry
* physically attack the person they think "made them" feel angry
* feel "numb" by not feeling anything at all
* EXPLODE over small situations (e.g. rush hour driving)

I will never forget my very first workshop, which I led at an alternative high school 6 years ago. It was with a group of 10 teenagers who were juvenile delinquents–some of whom had been in jail, others, on probation. I had created and developed a program for teens, titled "Mission Possible: Building Healthy Self-Esteem," on self-esteem, motivation, goal setting and anger. I had tried to make it as creative as possible by including tons of music, improvisation-acting and a variety of art.

I remember feeling extremely uncomfortable for several reasons. First, I was only 2 years older than most of the youth. Second, their body language was not inviting. The teens were sitting on sofas arranged in a circle, and no one even looked at me. There were 8 guys, most of whom were wearing hoods on their heads, some wearing sunglasses, and others just staring at the floor. I had no eye contact at all. There were 2 girls. One was quiet and never spoke. The other, Natasha, wore a black lacy bra, was fully body pierced and had several tattoos. Natasha had a real presence and spunk about her. She was definitely the leader of the group. When she talked, everyone listened.

I was petrified! I had just spent 3 months designing this workshop but had no idea how youth would relate to it. For the first hour, none of the guys even looked up at me. I think most of them were doodling on some paper. The 2 girls would occasionally give me eye contact.

Then I did this activity called "Name That Feeling." This is a game to see how music impacts on our feelings. I played 8 different popular songs, each for 15 seconds, and they were to write down how they felt during the playing. There was a wide range in music styles from alternative to hard rock to hip hop to country. I played music they liked, and some they definitely didn't like.

I collected the anonymous answer sheets and read them out loud. Surprisingly, the major feeling that was mentioned was **anger**. If I played hip hop music, they felt angry. If I played alternative music, they felt angry. No matter what the music was, the angry feelings showed up on their sheets. This told me that anger was a feeling very familiar to them!

At the end of the workshop, I was exhausted. I remember thinking to myself the workshop was a complete failure. The teacher certainly didn't help my confidence. He typed out 15-20 things that "didn't work" in the workshop. I felt insecure about my abilities and wanted to go run and hide somewhere.

Interestingly enough, Natasha, the leader of the group, stayed behind waiting for her bus. She overheard her teacher give me his negative feedback. Then he asked her, "So, Natasha, what did you think about the workshop?" She said, "Are you kidding? It was awesome! That part on anger was amazing! I think we've all exploded or felt numb. It all made sense! We needed to hear that." The teacher and I looked equally surprised. I can honestly say that if it were not for Natasha's comment, I don't know where I would be right now! Her positive comment fuelled my motivation to improve my workshops, while her honest reply about anger showed me the need for understanding anger.

Anger is a Sign for Hurt, Sad or Frustrated.

Anger Is a Signal

Think of anger as an emotional **stop** sign or as a secondary emotion. It's a signal that we are feeling hurt, sad or frustrated. But most of us wouldn't say, "I'm so hurt," because we would fear coming across as vulnerable and weak. So, instead, we often say, "You piss me off."

"Pissed off" really means angry, and angry means hurt, sad and/or frustrated. But most of us will say, "pissed off" because it sounds stronger and tougher. It's covering up our true feelings.

So next time you're feeling angry, be **HONEST** and ask yourself, "Am I feeling hurt, sad or frustrated?" Try to be honest with yourself!

The Jar of Feelings

I explained the dynamics of anger to this alternative high school youth group by holding up a jar of candy. "In my jar, I have two colours of candy, red and black. The red candies represent pleasant feelings (e.g., happy, excited). The black candies represent **unpleasant** feelings (e.g., angry, sad, hurt, frustrated)." I shared with the group that we all have this jar of positive and negative feelings inside of us. The question is, do we have more pleasant or unpleasant feelings in this jar? And do we put a lid on the jar if there are too many negative feelings?

When we keep putting unpleasant 'candies' in our jar, the jar starts getting really full. When the jar starts getting close to full, one of two things will happen: (1) An Explosion, or (2) Feeling Numb.

(1) The Explosion (e.g.,Road Rage)

Pleasant feelings are easy to deal with. I don't think any of us would complain about feeling happy or excited. However, unpleasant feelings are more difficult to deal with. Feelings we cannot control, but our reaction to them is a choice, and we can control our words and actions. For example, if a friend of mine does something that hurts me, I have to make a decision on how to deal with it. It's as though she has just handed me a black candy. I'm holding it now, but what am I going to do with it? Usually how I deal with my feelings depends on my communication style. If I'm Blind and passive-aggressive, I probably would **PRETEND** it doesn't really bother me. Or I may tell another of my friends about it. In both those cases, it's as though I'm putting that black candy in my jar. But remember, once our jar starts getting really full, it's only a matter of time before it gets too full and we "**explode.**"

Kurt was a 17-year-old referred to me by his parents. His parents told me that he had "problems communicating and dealing with anger." Kurt had a pattern of keeping everything bottled up, not talking with his parents and then "exploding." When I met with Kurt, I didn't ask him if he was angry. I **asked** him, "What's happening in your life that frustrates you?" At first he made comments such as "Nothing," and "I don't like it when my mom asks me to do stuff, but it's not really a big deal." The more we talked I understood that it was not one main thing that frustrated Kurt, but many small situations that were explained as "no big deal." But when the small situations were all added up, his jar would get full and he would explode. He told me about the time that his mom asked him to do the dishes, when he was watching TV. Usually he would just ignore her comment, say nothing, then complain to his friends. But that day, his emotional jar was full of black candies, and her comment was the "last straw." He freaked, **SCREAMING** at her and punching walls. Underlying all this anger was a lot of built-up frustration. He didn't know what his parents expected of him. They would randomly say, "Do this or do that," and they expected it done immediately. Small frustrations would be ignored, build up and later explode into a big fight. How Kurt was dealing with his anger was greatly impacting his relationship with his parents.

ROAD RAGE is a common example of built-up anger exploding. I remember one particular time driving in Toronto on my way to a meeting. To summarize, there was major construction, it was 5:00 p.m. rush hour and everyone was bumper to bumper. I was as frustrated as everyone else, especially when I knew I was going to be late. I was stopped at a red light when the car beside me was rear-ended by another car from behind. It wasn't a major collision, but there was definite damage. I sat there in my car and observed this drama. The guy whose car was hit got out of his car and went to other car. Opening the car door, he took the driver out by grabbing his face, threw him on the ground, and started punching and kicking him. I sat there frozen, not knowing what I should be doing. These two guys were punching each other and rolling on the ground. They started rolling around the front of my car. The light turned green, but of course I couldn't move; otherwise, I would have run right over them. I quickly **LOCKED** my doors and watched this grown man attack the other. They rolled around to my side of the car. I felt like rolling down my window and saying, "Buddy, you've got some serious built-up anger," but I decided not to in fear of what he might do. Once the light turned green again, and they rolled behind my car, I took off. The police were on their way. Someone else must have called the police during this rumble around my car. In this type of situation, it is best to call for help to protect yourself and others around you.

The attacker was obviously Disguised and aggressive. He verbally and physically attacked the guy whose car had hit his. His jar of feelings was full of frustration! The fact that his car was hit was the last straw, and he "lost it." His actions were out of proportion to the provocation! He was not acting out his frustration over only one situation. He was acting out over all the frustrated feelings that were in his jar. As a result, he probably got an assault charge and possibly a criminal record.

I am not surprised how road rage is growing. When you think about it, it's a safe place to vent anger, at people we don't know. We may swear, use offensive gestures, chase or verbally attack the "bad drivers." And we need never see them again. We don't know who they are, and they don't know who we are. However, road rage is causing some **SEVERE** accidents. According to the American Automobile Association, road rage has been on the increase by 7% since 1990. In the U.K., a study by Lex Research reported that of Britain's 2.8 million company car drivers, 83% have been victims of some sort of road rage during their working life. Eighteen percent have been physically threatened by another driver, while 21% reported having been run off the road.

(2) Feeling Numb (the Feeling Switch Is Off)

When our jar of feelings is full, turning the feeling switch off or feeling numb is another way that many people cope with angry feelings.

The first time I heard of numbness was when I was 17 years old. I was dating a guy who at the time had undergone a lot of difficulties. He had experienced unemployment, career difficulties, family and friend conflicts. When I asked him how he was feeling, he said, "Actually, I don't really feel anything. I feel totally **numb**." I didn't know what he was talking about. How could anyone not feel anything?

As I look back, I think he was Blind. He had received many black candies and continually put them in his jar. When his jar got too full of these unpleasant feelings, he put the lid tightly on the jar. He shut off his feeling switch. He would rather feel numb than experience unpleasant feelings. Some people might see this as being alright. Keeping the lid on the jar keeps us from feeling unpleasant feelings. However, it also keeps us from feeling pleasant feelings. We can't experience joy or peace or true happiness when our feeling switch is off.

When I was 21 years old, another of my friends told me about her numbness. I went out for dinner with one of my closest friends, Maggie. Maggie's mom had died recently, and it was the first time I had seen her since the funeral. I asked her how she was doing, and she responded, "Actually, I'm fine. I don't feel anything–kind of numb." She then continued, telling me about some recent outrageous decisions that did not sound like the Maggie I knew. She was partying pretty hard, cheating on her boyfriend and lying to her family and friends. I felt as if I were talking to a stranger, someone I didn't know. This behaviour was so unlike Maggie.

I shared with Maggie the danger of feeling numb. Our feelings are a **signal**. They help us. For example, I have feeling in my hand when I put my hand on a hot stove element, a terrible physical pain that is an urgent signal to move my hand so it won't burn. The opposite often happens when we are numb. If I feel numb, I enter an "I don't care" phase. Then, feelings no longer are a signal to prompt us to make good decisions. Instead, we often make decisions that hurt us and other people. It is so important that we turn on our feeling signal, be prepared to experience the unpleasant feelings, and deal with them, so that we can move on with our lives and experience pleasant feelings as well.

DEALING WITH ANGER:
The Lifers may

* be assertive with their anger
* confront the person they are angry towards
* not attack or blame the other person for their feelings
* take ownership or claim responsibility for their part in a conflict situation
* express their feelings of sadness, hurt and frustration through talking, art, poetry or sports
* express their feelings not to attempt to change some one else, but to let their own point of view be known
* recognise that their feelings and thoughts are equally important as those of others

When I first started working with Kurt (mentioned in the explosion section) he was passive-aggressive and aggressive with his anger. He bottled up his feelings, then exploded. He often blamed the whole situation on his parents.

I shared with Kurt that he has every right to feel frustrated towards his parents. And his parents have every right to feel frustrated towards him. **FEELING** frustration is very different from acting out frustration. His feelings are important, and they need to be heard. But when they were acted out, they weren't being heard! His mom especially would shut down and become very quiet when she sensed his aggressive tone of voice coming.

For part of our counselling time Kurt and I focussed on how he communicates his anger or frustration to his parents. I challenged him to go home and say, "Mom, Dad, I can understand that you want certain jobs done, and I know you do a lot for me. But I feel frustrated when you tell me what to do and expect it done immediately. I would appreciate it if at the beginning of the week you would tell me what is expected of me so I can plan out my week. My time is important to me." When we talked about this in my office, he was rolling his eyes and said, "Karyn, there's no way I can say that to my parents. They won't listen. They won't change." But the goal of being assertive with our feelings is not to change the other person. The goal is to let our feelings and thoughts be known. When we are assertive, we're **sticking** up for ourselves, communicating the best we can so that the receiver will actually listen. Communicating assertively doesn't mean the person will change or agree with us, but at least we know we've done our part.

So Kurt took up the challenge. He went home and, that evening, his parents yelled at him to do a chore immediately. He said, "Dad, it really hurts me when you ask me to do something right away. It makes me feel as if my time is not as important as your time." Kurt said his dad's jaw literally dropped. His dad was so surprised that he didn't say anything for about two minutes. Then he replied, "I know your time is **IMPORTANT** but the lawn needs to get done." So Kurt suggested, "I'll do it for you. But do you mind if I finish watching this show, and then I'll do it right after?" His father agreed.

Kurt came in to see me the following week with a huge grin. He was so proud of himself that he'd done it. He told me honestly, "Karyn, I really didn't think it would work! But I felt so good about myself, and that I was being the mature one. I felt that my dad actually listened to me, which was the first time in a long time!"

Similarly, my friend Maggie learned to turn on her feeling switch and be more assertive with her anger. As I mentioned in the "Feeling Numb" section, Maggie felt numb. Her jar of feelings was completely **FULL** so she turned off the switch. Inside that jar of feelings were many sad and hurt feelings about her mother's death.

For Maggie to turn on her feeling switch, she needed to realise what she was feeling. After many hours of talking she realised that she had intense feelings of sadness and grief because of her mom's death. She also recognised that she was frustrated with her dad, for remarrying within 1 year of her mother's death, frustrated that she **lost** her room at her parents' house because of her two new step-siblings, and frustrated with her boyfriend for not "being there" for her. Instead of attacking others or blaming them for her problems, she started to face her feelings head-on. She started talking about her mom, keeping a journal, visiting the gravesite, and allowing herself to be sad instead of being the "strong one." After several months, she confronted her dad with her feelings of frustration and sadness that he'd remarried so quickly. She didn't attack him, but focussed on her feelings.

Slowly, Maggie confronted her feelings instead of avoiding them or blaming someone for them. This process, she would tell you, was difficult and took months, but was incredibly rewarding.

Dear Karyn,

I hate both my stepfather and my stepmother. Every day, at my dad's house, I get yelled at. My stepmother yelled that I should learn not to be grumpy all the time, but it's hard with her yelling at me all the time. Last week I cleaned the whole house since I was really bored; then she yelled at me when my brother left the porch light on. I felt like yelling at her to shut up. She also won't let me get the money I saved up off of my dad.

My stepfather yells at me whenever I'm at my mom's house. I take care of all my siblings, all the time, and I do a lot of work (more than everybody else in the house together). I do the dishes, prepare meals, clean the house a lot, go grocery shopping, and I still get yelled at for not doing any work. He yells, saying I get and eat too many treats, but I practically starve myself. I'm a vegetarian and whenever I go over there, he makes meat meals that I don't like, and he forces me to eat them. (I get sick after.) I really need help-I think I hate my stepparents.

Blueh

Dear Blueh,

Sounds extremely frustrating! I don't blame you for feeling angry towards your stepparents. It doesn't sound like they understand you. This is a tough situation, but here are my suggestions.

First, remember that you can't change them, you can only change yourself. I know you've probably heard that line before, but the cliche speaks truth! The only thing you can do is focus on yourself, your attitude and your actions. The more you focus on how irritating their behaviour is, the more frustrated you will feel. So focus on yourself. How do you respond when they yell? Do you yell or swear back? Sounds like they know how to push your buttons. What are your buttons, and how do you respond when they are pushed?

Second, think in advance about how you want to respond to them. If you act aggressively (i.e., yelling, swearing) chances are you will be punished or grounded. Plus, I doubt they will hear what you are saying. Most people, myself included, tune out when others are aggressive. We naturally get defensive, and the argument heightens.

Third, be honest with yourself. Is there any truth to what your stepparents are saying? Are you often grumpy? What is your responsibility in the arguments? Could you handle it differently? If you really want to be mature, **admit your part of the argument.** *This is very tough, but it shows extreme maturity and honesty!*

So before the next argument happens, think about how you want to respond. What would you like to say? How do you want to say it? How we talk is extremely important! Practise your new response. Be prepared. Think of this new response as a shield. You are protecting yourself against their negative comments. No longer will you allow your buttons to be pushed. When the next argument happens, speak your mind, assertively. Say, calmly, what you think and feel. If they hear it and respond with open arms, great! If not, know that you behaved maturely and did your part! Talking assertively builds self-esteem. So I hope you feel good about yourself, knowing that you handled yourself well!

We all feel angry at times - that's just part of being human. Feeling anger is healthy, but how we deal with it can be destructive. Anger can control us when we don't control it. So it is important to find healthy ways to get the anger out! Some like talking, others like writing and doing art as a creative way to express themselves. The important thing is to find a creative way or space for you to express your thoughts and feelings. By your doing this, your anger will most likely decrease and so will your grumpiness.

Finally, it doesn't sound like your stepparents are supportive of you. So I highly suggest you look for another parental figure or mentor who can offer you this support. Someone who can really encourage and love you unconditionally! Maybe this is another relative, perhaps a teacher, maybe even the parent of a friend. The bottom line is, we all need people we can look up to and who challenge us! Everyone needs at least one person like *this in their life. Life can be frustrating and disappointing, and we all need support.*

❀ ❀ ❀

Remember that you are valuable! Just because you may not feel loved by your stepparents doesn't mean that they don't care about you or that you are unlovable. We are all lovable, so surround yourself with people who truly care about you!

Karyn xl

Published in the national Canadian magazine *What*, June 2001.

SECOND BASE: The Impact
How does your attitude about yourself affect how you perceive your body?

BODY IMAGE:
The Blind & Disguised may
* work towards the "Quick Fix," working only on their body image to feel good about themselves
* under-eat or overeat to feel control in their life
* starve themselves or decrease their food intake as punishment when they have not achieved a goal
* eat when depressed or upset to feel better
* spend hours on getting ready, aiming for the "perfect hair, makeup and outfit"
* be extremely fussy about wearing only designer label clothes

* be consumed with diet plans and workout strategies
* believe teasing or negative comments about their body image from their peers, even though the comments are not true (e.g., a girl gets called 'fat' and therefore thinks she's fat)[xli]

STATISTICS

* In the U.S., 80% of women are dissatisfied with their bodies.[xlii]
* Most models are thinner than 98% of women in the U.S.[xliii]
* In the U.S., 5-10 million girls and women and 1 million boys and men struggle with an eating disorder.[xliv]
* Approximately 45% of American women and 25% of American men are on a diet on any given day.[xlv]

For the record, there is nothing wrong with wanting to take care of one's body image by being physically fit, exercising properly, wearing designer label clothes, going on a diet and working out. The question is, does this **CONTROL** you or do you control it? What is your motivation? As mentioned earlier, so many of us aim for the "Quick Fix," the conditional self-esteem that says, "I will feel good about myself if . . ." Often the excuses are related to the body image. The unrealistic belief is, "If I look good, I will feel good, and I will impress people." It may work for a short time period, but it doesn't last.

Daniela, a 15-year-old client, sat in my office, trying to **PERSUADE** me that she was fat. She was exactly the opposite-very slim! Daniela had a petite frame, was 5 feet 4 inches tall, and weighed only 100 pounds. When she confidently told me, "Karyn, I'm fat, and I want to lose 10 pounds"–I knew something else was going on in her life. Her obsession with losing weight led her to stop eating, and start taking laxatives. This resulted in her mood often becoming irritable and unhappy. There are millions of "Danielas" in North America.

The opposite to Daniela's problem occurred in another teen I counselled, 19-year-old Patricia. Patricia's pattern was to eat when she was upset. If she felt down or depressed, she would walk to the kitchen and begin eating. She was approximately 30 pounds overweight and desperately wanted to lose the weight.

When I met with Patricia, she was depressed because she had gained so much weight. Yet when she was feeling **depressed** about her weight, she would turn to food. I asked her, "What would happen if you did lose the weight? Who would be the happiest?" Surprisingly, she did not say herself. She said, "My mother would be the most thrilled, because she would think it was all her doing." Patricia then shared with me her relationship with her mother, who was very image oriented. All that mattered for her mother was how someone looked. Who cares about their feelings, or what's inside . . . do they look good? When Patricia was 13 years old and starting to gain a bit of weight, her mother put her on laxatives and would not give her as much food as her siblings. Her mother also made comments such as "No guys will ever like you at that weight." Her mother obviously was very controlling and wanted Patricia to have the "perfect body." The more Patricia's mother wanted her to lose weight, the more Patricia would eat.

Food represented control for Patricia. Her mom used food to control her. So Patricia used food to control her mother. When Patricia ate, she was showing her mom, passively aggressively, "Mom, you can't control me! I am in control of myself."

When we look more closely at the situation, however, Patricia was being controlled by her mother, but in the opposite way. Patricia was doing the reverse of what her mother wanted, therefore still being controlled. When I asked Patricia, "What do you want for you, not for your mother?" she said, "I want to be a **healthy** weight." So for most of her counselling, we tried to focus on what Patricia wanted for herself and figuring out a workout plan for her. Part of our work together was also learning to be assertive towards her mother.

Girls and guys handle body image differently. While girls may under-eat or overeat, guys may become obsessed with working out and developing muscles. I remember at high school all the talk about steroids, and which guys used them.

Again, there is nothing wrong with working out and aiming to be physically fit. But what is your motivation? Do you think, "If I get to this weight or this size, I will be happy"? Then, once again, our self-esteem is conditional. And if our self-esteem is dependent on our being the right weight, or having the most impressive physique, obviously there is a lot of pressure to get that weight and muscle power. When the stakes are high, we often will do whatever it takes to reach that goal, including taking steroids.

A friend of mine, Greg, is Disguised. He puts other people down. To elevate himself, he focuses on his body weight. The first time I went to his place, I noticed *Men's Fitness* magazines everywhere. Obviously, there is nothing wrong with the magazine, but Greg talked about it non-stop. He talked about his weight, what weight he would like to be, his workout plan–everything. We all talk about things that are important to us, and for Greg that was his body image. He told me that he was in a car accident 2 years earlier, and because of the treatment, he said, "I lost a lot of my muscle weight, and my self-esteem went down with it." Greg's self-esteem was **attached** to the size of his muscles. Because he was physically smaller now, he felt inferior. As a result, he talked excessively with me about weight. If I tried to change the topic, only moments later he would revert back to talk of himself and his body image.

BODY IMAGE:
The Lifers often

* work towards the "Inside-Out"
* want to attain a **HEALTHY** weight for themselves
* want to take care of their appearance, but their appearance doesn't control them
* **ACCEPT** what they cannot change, and work on what they can change

The key difference between the Blind/Disguised and the Lifers is that the Lifers work towards the Inside-Out, focussing first on their personality and strengths. The outside appearance is secondary. It's important for all of us to take care of ourselves. That means enhancing our appearance, not our appearance controlling us!

For example, can you feel good about yourself if you are in public **without** any makeup, without bragging about your muscle weight gain, without wearing the perfect clothes? If not, your body image might be the pivot for your self-esteem.

Even up to a couple of years ago, there was no way I could go out in public without makeup on. Remember, there is nothing wrong with makeup, but was it a **crutch** for my self-esteem? I would say yes. Now, I'm at the point where I can go out in public with or without it. I may want to wear makeup, but I don't need it to feel comfortable and at ease. I remember the first time I deliberately went out in public without it. I was very self-conscious at first. But I proved to myself it no longer controlled me. It was a very liberating feeling!

Last year, I produced a video about self-esteem, and I interviewed teens across North America to have them "spill their guts" on this issue. One teenaged girl, slightly overweight, from Kansas City, said to me, "I'm happy about who I am. I don't feel the need to lose weight for myself or anybody else. I know my body shape is not perfect, but that's OK. I've accepted what I've got."

The Lifers accept what they cannot change about their body image and **work** on what they can change! Acceptance is the key!

Dear Karyn,

I have a really close friend I have known my whole life, and a couple of years back, she had an eating disorder of bingeing and purging. It was scary for everybody, and she never got any medical help because she thought she could stop it on her own. She is a strong girl, and we all believed she could do it. Now, we are seeing signs that she is starting again. We want a way of talking to her without making it look like we are accusing her and making her feel bad. We don't want to upset her; we just want her to get better. I was wondering if you had any advice for me on what I should do about the situation.

NH

Dear NH,

Sounds like you are really concerned for your friend, and I don't blame you. Eating disorders are very serious and dangerous. Personally, I've had several friends who have had eating disorders, so I understand how frustrating and scary it can be.

Eating disorders generally have nothing to do with food. Food isn't the problem, but a sign of a larger one. Often, people with a disorder have lost control somewhere in their life. Feeling confused and helpless, they turn to bingeing and purging to regain a sense of control. When they starve or purge, they feel temporarily powerful and in control. But over time, their solution turns into the problem-and it can have deadly consequences.

Eating disorders are more common with teens who have a low self-esteem. Yet bingeing often starts as a way to cope with parents' divorce, a relationship breakup, abuse or controlling parents. The possibilities are endless. The root problem needs to be uncovered; otherwise, this habit will probably continue.

The first step is to let her know how much you care about her and that you are one of her supports. Get her talking about her feelings. Does she feel angry, sad, out of control? She needs to start talking about her feelings instead of acting on them. You're right-she may get upset with you. But that is the price for truly caring about your friend's well-being.

Secondly, it's extremely important she talk with a doctor about her bingeing. Bingeing and purging cause great damage to the body. After she has seen a doctor, I highly recommend that she find a counsellor trained in eating disorders. Her doctor would be able to suggest one. She needs to talk about her feelings and discover what is really causing her to binge. It is important that she is accountable to someone-other than you-otherwise, this situation may become overwhelming for her and you.

You mentioned that she is a "strong girl". I used to think that being strong and independent was healthy. But that's not necessarily the case. We need to learn to be interdependent, which means learning to depend on others at certain times. It takes strength to ask for help. And we all need help at certain points in our life.

If your friend still refuses to go for help after you share this with her, I highly recommend you tell a parent or guardian you trust. This could be your parent, her parent, a guidance counsellor or a teacher. I understand that telling an adult might seem like violating loyalty or trust. However, the only time I feel it's necessary to divulge secrets is when someone is harming themselves or someone else. This is called "tough love" and means you care so much for your friend that you risk her being angry with you for the sake of her safety. And at this point, it's more important that she's safe than not angry.

You sound like a supportive friend. The truth is, she needs to get help. I challenge you to take this risk and focus on her safety. This is a true test of friendship.

Sincerely,
Karyn[xlvi]

Published in the national Canadian magazine *What*, February 2001.

SECOND BASE: The Impact
How is your attitude about yourself affected if your parents' divorce?

DEALING WITH PARENTS' DIVORCE:
The Blind & Disguised may

* **BLAME** themselves (the Blind)
* blame or attack (verbally or physically) their parents (the Disguised)
* feel angry towards one or both parents
* express their feelings aggressively towards their parents
* keep all their feelings inside (passive)
* feel a lack of security in their environment and themselves
* feel **abandoned**
* get a lack of attention from their parents
* feel the divorce is their fault
* think that their parents don't love them
* think that they have lost one or both parents

If our parents divorce, it is a circumstance that we can't control. It just happens. This circumstance often greatly impacts our self-esteem, however. Think about it–our family is our foundation. Overnight, this security is stripped away. Our identity stems from our family and if that is removed, it often leaves us hanging emotionally.

How much a divorce impacts our self-esteem depends on how highly our self-esteem was DEVELOPED before it happens. If we're Blind or Disguised, we tend to blame our parents or ourselves. If we're a Lifer, we tend to understand that it's a choice made by our parents; it has nothing to do with us, although we're obviously greatly affected. Handling divorce is never pleasant, and it definitely tests our inner securities.

I counselled a 17-year-old girl named Melissa. Melissa at first felt that her parents' divorce was her fault. She told me, "I used to wonder whether if I had behaved better they might not have divorced. Maybe I was too much of a problem kid. I blamed myself and hated myself more because of it. Then I realised something. Screw them! It's their fault, and they've "screwed up" my life. Do my parents have any idea what they've done to me? I don't know who I am! I don't have any self-esteem, and it's **all** their fault. They have screwed up my life. If they were going to get a divorce, why did they have to get married in the first place? And why did they have to have me? I'm never going to have kids to put them through this life. Why should I?"

Melissa was Disguised before the divorce. The divorce didn't change her self-esteem, but it did reinforce it negatively. She externalised or **BLAMED** her parents for "screwing up" her life. She chose to blame her parents for her lack of self-esteem. There's no question that the divorce impacted how she felt about herself. But she blamed all her problems on her parents' divorce.

When I asked Melissa how she felt about herself before the divorce she said, "I was just starting to figure myself out when I heard about the breakup. Teenagers have enough to deal with, without having to listen to their parents argue, play messenger between parents, move every week to another house . . . . It's too much." She was angry at first, but because she never dealt with it, the anger turned into bitterness. This bitterness led to a depression and lack of motivation. Melissa was aggressive about her feelings (like the Disguised)–and instead of dealing with her anger and sad feelings, she focussed on blaming her "screwed-up life" on her parents.

DEALING WITH PARENTS' DIVORCE:
The Lifers may
* feel **SAD** and hurt that their parents have divorced
* understand that their parents' divorce is **NOT** their fault
* think that they have two parents who care about them

As I stated earlier, generally divorce won't change our self-esteem. It will just reinforce feelings we have already. The more secure we are, the better we can handle the fallout from the divorce. But, obviously, divorce is never easy to deal with.

I counselled David, a 13-year-old whose parents had recently divorced. When I asked him how he was doing, he genuinely responded, "I'm sad. I wish they were together. I'm angry at how my dad talked to my mom, and I've told him." David knew it wasn't his fault. He didn't blame himself, nor did he blame his parents. He knew it was a choice that they'd made.

One aspect that amazed me about David was how assertive he was towards his dad. He bluntly told his dad how angry and upset he was with his behaviour. He didn't attack his dad but ASSERTIVELY said, "Dad, I felt frustrated when you talked to Mom like that." Talk about maturity! He was clearly a Lifer. He was assertive with his feelings and voiced them when necessary. He knew his opinion was important. He was secure enough within himself to know that he was going to make it through this adjustment even though he was hurting.

He also assertively told his dad that it was not his responsibility to play messenger between his parents. His dad would frequently ask him to give a message or package to his mom. His parents were continually fighting and had major difficulties communicating. Yet David understood that their marriage problems were not his problems. They are two adults and therefore quite capable of sorting out the daily details of raising their teens. David set his boundaries by assertively saying, "Dad, I understand that you don't like talking with Mom, but I feel really frustrated when I'm asked to play messenger. I don't believe that is my role or responsibility as a teen. You're both adults. I think that talking to Mom is your responsibility." Fortunately, his dad, although quite shocked by his comments, understood where David was coming from and stopped asking David to play the middleman. David felt **RELIEVED** after this discussion because he focussed on what he could control, his response to his parents! As a result, his relationship with his dad actually improved!

SECOND BASE: The Impact
How does your attitude about yourself affect peer presure?

DEALING WITH PEER PRESSURE:
The Blind may
* find it **difficult** to say "No" (to the pressure of drugs, sex, smoking, alcohol)
* say "No," but then still give in to the pressure

* agree to the pressure just to fit in and belong to the group
* need a place to belong and therefore will do whatever it takes

Let me just say that peer pressure doesn't stop at the teenager stage. As long as we have peers, there tends to be pressure. The question is, How do we handle it? For the Blind, saying no is often difficult. As mentioned in the communication section, the Blind are passive-aggressive. So, if they don't want to do something, they may tell a third person, but rarely stick up for themselves. If the Blind have the strength to say no, their **values** about that pressure are so strong that even their insecurities won't knock them over.

One of my first clients when I started my counselling practice was a 14-year-old girl named Andrea. Andrea had undergone more than some of us would in our entire life. Her mom was an alcoholic and therefore "not around." Andrea was responsible for cooking, cleaning, doing laundry and looking after her younger brother. She was never good enough for her mother, who constantly put her down to the point that Andrea was clearly Blind. To handle the stress, she started drinking, like her mother. A couple of years later she was at a party and pot was being passed around. She felt indifferent towards pot, so why not try it? "Pot," she said, "helped me take my mind off my problems." It helped her relax. At another party, she was offered harder drugs. She didn't really want to try them, but saying no seemed to be too **embarrassing**. After all, these were her friends. How could she say no? By the time I met Andrea, at age 14, she was dating a guy 19 years old, and doing drugs with this guy almost daily. She had lost her virginity to him. She said, "I was hoping he would love me." Instead he took off. The only things she was left with were her low self-esteem and her drug addiction.

DEALING WITH PEER PRESSURE:
The Disguised may
* **PRESSURE** others into doing what they want (drugs, sex, smoking, alcohol)
* find it difficult to say no to the pressure
* like to CONTROL others and therefore ignore it when someone else says no

---

People try different things for different reasons. Just because someone tries drugs doesn't mean that they are Blind or Disguised. For some, it's curiosity. For others, it's a coping mechanism to help them take their mind off their problems.

I don't want to generalise here, but it's important to know that everyone handles situations DIFFERENTLY. Obviously, we need to look at individual cases and see the MOTIVATION for their behaviour.

But certain behaviours can <u>sometimes</u> be predicted. The Disguised want to control and put us down, especially in social settings.

Remember, in the body language chapter I wrote about the three brothers, Derek (the eldest), whom I analysed, John (in the middle) and Jeff (the youngest)? Derek was clearly Disguised. I remember watching him order liquor shots for his younger brothers. John kept saying no, but then when the shots arrived he would drink them. Derek paid **NO** attention to his brother's answer. All he cared about was that his brothers got drunk. As for Jeff, he happily took the free drinks.

Derek's controlling behaviour towards his brothers is filtered towards women as well. I remember sitting at my table, in this café in Israel, still waiting for my friend, while talking with the three brothers, when the waiter passed by. Derek said, "Mate, would you bring the lovely lady a glass of red wine?" while pointing **towards** me. Some might see that as sweet or nice. I saw it as controlling. He hadn't asked me whether or not I wanted a drink. He hadn't asked me if I even liked wine. I looked at the waiter and said, "Actually, cancel that order. I don't feel like wine right now." Derek turned to the waiter and repeatedly said, "Would you get a drink for the woman?" Now he was being very controlling. I looked back at the waiter and said, "Cancel that order. I don't want a drink. If this guy had actually asked me, instead of ordering for me, he might have figured that out." The poor waiter's head was going back and forth, as though he were WATCHING a tennis match. Derek had the nerve to make his request one more time. "The lady really wants it. She's just playing hard to get. Bring the wine." Now I was ticked off. I looked at Derek and said, "If you want the wine for yourself, fine. But I don't want it." It was evident he wanted to get me drinking. Derek eventually ordered the wine for himself, and then gave it to me. I gave it back to him. The wine sat untouched on his table for the rest of the night. It was a very annoying **SYMBOL** of his trying to control me, and my not giving in to it. Remember, anytime you say no and someone ignores the no or tries to change your mind, they are trying to control you!

DEALING WITH PEER PRESSURE:
The Lifers often

* KNOW what they want and don't want as it relates to sex, drugs, alcohol and smoking
* say "No" to peer pressure because they are confident with who they are
* do not encourage others to do or try something that they don't want to
* respect it when others say "No"

Dealing with peer pressure is never easy! The main difference between the Disguised/Blind and the Lifers is how they deal with that pressure. The Disguised often like to control others, the Blind often give in to the pressure, while the Lifers learn to say yes to what they want and no to what they don't want.

There are a few options for **DEALING** with pressure. One option is to avoid situations where you think there will be pressure. However, there are usually Disguised at parties, trying to pressure others, and who wants to be avoiding parties for the rest of their life? So, in my mind, the best way is to learn how to say no, and choose friends who will respect your answer!

Remember this simple rule: When you say "No," and someone ignores it, they are trying to control you. The fact that Derek wanted to buy me a drink was nice, by itself. However, the "niceness" turned controlling and manipulative very quickly. When I said "No," he **ignored** my request 3 times. He then ordered it anyway, hoping I would drink it when it arrived. I didn't touch it. I **CHOSE** not to be manipulated.

It's important for the Lifers not only to say "No," but to stick with it, and not give in. Otherwise your "No" seems useless after a while. Derek's middle brother figured that out. He kept saying no, but then when his drinks arrived, he would drink them. So obviously Derek learned to disregard his brother's "No," which encouraged Derek in the future to keep controlling him.

Saying "No" is incredibly POWERFUL for three reasons. First, it means we stick up for ourselves and build our assertiveness and self-esteem. It's showing yourself and others around you that you know what you want, that you know what you don't want, and that you believe your opinion matters. You are confident about your values, and it shows. Second, it prevents people from "walking" all over you and getting you to do what they want. Andrea, mentioned in the Blind section, knew this all too well. How differently would Andrea's life have gone if she had learned how to say "No"? Probably much differently. Finally, when we say "No," we gain self-respect, and often others will gain respect for us. People generally don't respect doormats or those who don't stick up for themselves.

SECOND BASE: The Impact
How is your attitude about yourself affected by abuse?

If there is one aspect of life that impacts on our self-esteem the most, it is abuse. Abuse, whether it is emotional, physical or sexual, greatly deteriorates any existing self-esteem. The healthier our attitude about ourselves is, the better we can deal with the impact of abuse. However, for thousands of North Americans, abuse STARTS in early childhood, before a healthy self-image has developed. For these individuals, the abuse will have the greatest consequences.

This chapter will look at symptoms of abuse, and how this impacts our self-esteem. If we have been abused, how does this AFFECT how we treat other people?

Abuse is a common word, easily thrown around, so let's clarify exactly what it is!

Emotional/Psychological Abuse

involves a **negative** comment, put-down, threat to harm someone, aiming to control the other person.

> Example: "You're stupid, and you're not going to amount to anything!"
> Example: "You're fat. No wonder you can't get anyone. Who would want you?"
> Example: "If you don't smarten up, I'm going to kill you!"

Physical Abuse

involves intentionally physically harming someone else.

> Examples: hitting, punching, scratching, biting, suffocating, burning, choking, stabbing, or throwing objects at (someone)

Sexual Abuse

involves touching, fondling someone in sexual areas.

> Examples: being touched in sexual areas; forced to have sex; fondled or kissed when such attention was unwanted; raped; told that all they were good for was sex; forced to perform oral sex; forced to pose for sexual photos; or to watch sexual videos

STATISTICS

* One million Canadian children have witnessed abuse against their mothers by their fathers or father figures.[xlvii]
* TWO-THIRDS of abuse occurs in the home or by someone that the victim trusts (i.e., parent, dating partner, teacher, friend, doctor, religious leader).[xlviii]
* Children who witness abuse in the home often show signs of stress, decline in their social skills and schoolwork.[xlix]
* In 1997, youth under 18 represented 24% of the population, but were 60% of all sexual abuse victims and 19% of physical abuse victims.[l]
* Victims in abusive relationships often stay in the relationship because of **LOW** self-esteem, shame, lack of support, fear for their life or thinking that they deserved the abuse.[li]
* In 1996, 48% of abuse was committed by males towards females; 39% of abuse was males towards males; 7% was females towards females; and 6% was females towards males.[lii]
* In a study of 111 female youths over 5 years, 23% admitted to sexual abuse by a date or boyfriend, 15% confessed unwanted sex with a date or boyfriend and 10% admitted to other kinds of sexual abuse, including being fondled and being forced to perform oral sex.[liii]
* One-third of teen relationships are abusive, as are similarly 1/3 of adult relationships.[liv]
* Thirty-six percent of teens reported abuse in their relationship.[lv]

DEALING WITH ABUSE:
The Blind may

* blame themselves for the abuse
* learn **not** to trust themselves and their intuition
* internalise the verbal abusive comments (If someone said, "You're stupid," they would think, "I'm stupid.")
* self-mutilate or self-inflict punishment
* try to protect the abuser, by hiding the physical abuse
* feel all they are good for is sex, if they were sexually abused
* become sexually promiscuous, because they believe they are only loved for sex
* have fear towards the abuser
* be **easily** controlled by the abuser, in fear of the consequences of not complying
* withdraw from other loved ones
* feel they are unlovable because the abuser does not love them
* view the abuser as a "god," believing everything that he/she says
* feel, as a consequence of the abuse, that they have little value
* be attracted to abusers as friends and relationship partners because that's what they are familiar with

Emotional, physical and sexual abuse TEND to have similar consequences. If someone, perhaps a child, is abused emotionally, physically or sexually, the first thing that happens is **loss** of ability to trust people. You may think, "Big deal! They'll get it back." But it's not that easy. Children naturally trust people, especially their parents and

137

guardians. But if their guardian abuses that trust, not only is the trust in the relationship gone, but also the child learns not to trust themselves. If we can't trust ourselves in making decisions, we often make poor decisions that could have huge consequences.

Being abused also increases the feeling of **FEAR**. In Third Base, I share about the importance of trying new things, to build healthy self-esteem. But if someone is fearful of trying new things, it becomes a major obstacle towards building a healthy self-concept.

If we have been mistreated, it greatly **IMPACTS** on our relationships. When we have a certain understanding of ourselves, it's like a blueprint. We'll go looking for other people to validate what we already know about ourselves. So, if I'm Blind and I think I'm stupid, even if 10 people tell me I'm smart I probably won't believe them, because what they say doesn't coincide with my current beliefs about myself. Instead, I will listen to the 1 person who tells me I'm stupid, because that matches what I currently believe.

It sounds crazy, but humans tend to stick to the familiar versus the unfamiliar at any cost. This explains why the abused often find themselves dating abusers. I hear comments such as, "I keep dating all the wrong guys. I'm a magnet for attracting abusive boyfriends." So often, it happens that the person abused by their parents finds a relationship partner who abuses them, unless the pattern is broken!

Sexual abuse is the most devastating abuse, with crucial consequences. The Blind, if used only for sex, will feel they are only good for sex. And if they think they are "only good for sex," they seek after it and may become sexually promiscuous. Of course, this in itself has consequences. One of the teens I counselled shared this with me: "I gave my virginity away to Bill this past year, because he was 18 years old, and he asked me for it. I thought about waiting longer but worried that he would leave. I loved him so much, I would do whatever he wanted. He told me he wanted to show me how much he loved me. I IMAGINED romantic music and red roses, just like in the movies. It wasn't like that at all. It was over before it ever started. I felt so disappointed and used. I felt like I gave myself away so cheaply. But I thought I would never have a guy like him unless I gave him what he wanted."

DEALING WITH ABUSE:
The Disguised may

* learn not to trust themselves and their intuition
* externalise verbal abusive comments (If someone said, "You're stupid", they would say, "Well, you're stupid.")
* try to protect the abuser, by hiding the physical abuse
* try to control others through sex (e.g., rape)
* become sexually promiscuous
* "show love" only through sex
* have fear towards the abuser
* be easily controlled by the abuser in fear of the consequences of not complying
* view the abuser as a "god," believing everything that he/she says
* feel, as a consequence of the abuse, that they have little value, yet they project that insecurity by acting as if they are better than everyone else
* be attracted to friends and relationship partners they can abuse (i.e., the Blind)

* abuse others in order to feel control, deal with bottled up anger or get revenge on someone who hurt them[lvi]

Remember that the Blind and Disguised feel the same underneath. They may experience the same abuse, yet they often handle it very differently. The Blind may blame themselves. The Disguised may blame everyone else. With emotional abuse, the Blind learn to put themselves down. The Disguised learned to put other people down, and therefore emotionally abuse others. With physical abuse, the Blind may feel they "deserved it," but the Disguised may start physically hurting other people. With sexual abuse, the Blind may learn they are only "valuable for sex" and therefore have sex with others, hoping to feel valuable. But, ironically enough, they feel even cheaper. The Disguised learn that sex means control. Since they were once controlled by their abuser, they may become a sex a buser themselves. The Disguised may try to increase their feeling of control in their life, by controlling and MANIPULATING others for sex. Disguised guys may try to use the right words to get what they want, "I'll love you if . . . ," or to turn a girl's "No," into "Yes" (i.e., date rape). Disguised girls may use their body, or wear sexy clothing, to control guys.

Outwardly, the Blind and Disguised are polar opposites. Inside, they often feel similarly lonely, victimised, fearful, distrustful and without value. Their abuser has put them down, controlled them and taken advantage of them. They have every reason to feel their negative feelings. However, when they start ACTING out their feelings, it often gets them into deeper trouble. The Blind act out their feelings on themselves (e.g., self-mutilation), and the Disguised act out their feelings on others (e.g., controlling and abusing others).

DEALING WITH ABUSE:
The Lifers may
* have learned through counselling or have read material about the impact of their abuse on their SELF-ESTEEM
* recognise that the abuse is not their fault
* learn to trust themselves and their intuition
* be assertive regarding verbal abusive comments (If someone said, "You are stupid," they would say, "Well, that's your opinion," or "I feel hurt when you say that.")
* tell someone about their abuser
* have fear towards the abuser
* try to avoid situations that might be abusive in order to PROTECT themselves
* not trust everything that the abuser says
* understand that they do have value, even though the abuser doesn't recognise that
* be attracted to friends and relationship partners who are kind, not abusive

---

As I mentioned earlier, gaining a healthier self-image is always possible! However, when it comes to the issue of abuse, I often get challenged. Many teens I've worked with think that their abuse will **permanently** lower their self-image. My response to them is, "It will, unless you ACKNOWLEDGE its impact and take action."

Many children who are abused grow up being Blind or Disguised, without even realising it. They've been put down, used, abused, and often think that's all they deserve.

But just because we think that's what we deserve it doesn't mean that it's true. The truth is that we all deserve to be treated equally and with respect! We all deserve to be loved! We all deserve to be aware of our strengths! We all deserve to be Lifers!

Stop and Think

The Lifers who have been abused have taken, at some point in their life, the time to Stop and Think! They have learned that the abuse was not their fault! They were the victims! They have learned that although the abuser acted tough and intimidating, the abuser was actually Disguised, controlling and abusing others due to their own lack of self-worth. The Lifers learn to begin the process of trusting themselves and their opinions. Practically speaking, they look at past situations and ask themselves, "What did I **LEARN** about myself?" or "How can I use that information to help me in my future?" They learn from their mistakes, instead of blaming others and repeating the same pattern. They learn to be assertive with people who are important to them, sticking up for their feelings and thoughts. Being assertive with abusive people may mean avoiding them, and taking care of oneself. The Lifers learn not to believe everything that their abuser has told them. Instead, they learn to Turn Up the **TRUTH** and Turn Off the Lies (Third Base). One of the greatest rewards of turning up the truth that the Lifers learn is to love themselves, perhaps for the first time. The more they learn to love themselves, the more they will be attracted to those who will also love them.

So Honestly Ask Yourself

Do you truly want to be a Lifer? Are you ready to really work at it? Do you expect this process to be easy? Do you think it will happen overnight? Do you think it's **POSSIBLE** to become a Lifer? The next Base will explain **FIVE** ways to get a grip on your life and your self-esteem!

THIRD BASE

The Steps

- • HOW CAN YOU FEEL GREAT ABOUT YOURSELF?
- • HOW CAN YOU HELP OTHERS FEEL GREAT ABOUT THEMSELVES?

STOP BLAMING, START OWNING AND CHANGING

* **STOP BLAMING:** What is your **responsibility?**
  What have you learned about
  yourself?
* **START OWNING:** How will you use this new
  information to better yourself?
  How will your **ATTITUDE**
  and behaviour change?

Think of this section as the framework or skeleton of self-esteem. These 5 steps are the skeleton or foundation that is needed to build a healthy and long-lasting sense of self. You can think of me as a coach; you are the one playing the game on the field. You might have absolutely the best coach in the world, but if players are not going to learn from their coach they will not grow and improve their game. I can't emphasize this enough: **YOU are the only one who can change your self-esteem!** I can't give it to you. Your parents can't give it to you. Your friends can't give it to you. Only you can, because self-esteem is an attitude and only you can choose what you want to believe.

I hope that at this point, after you've read the First and Second Bases, you know what your attitude is and how it's impacted your life. So now we launch into the steps to be more like the Lifers!

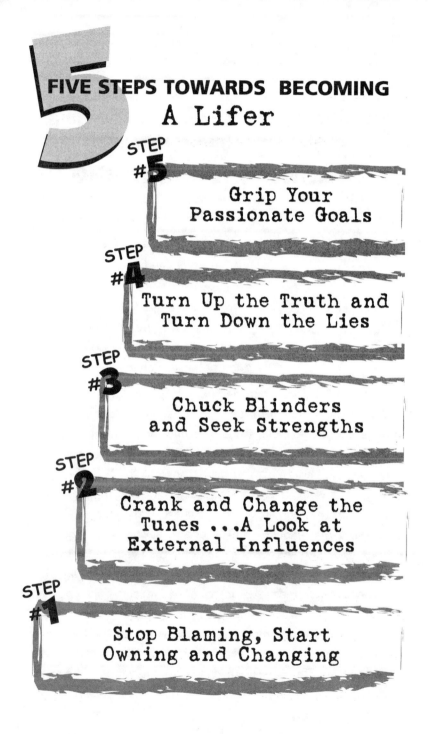

5 FIVE STEPS TOWARDS BECOMING
A Lifer

STEP #5
Grip Your Passionate Goals

STEP #4
Turn Up the Truth and Turn Down the Lies

STEP #3
Chuck Blinders and Seek Strengths

STEP #2
Crank and Change the Tunes ...A Look at External Influences

STEP #1
Stop Blaming, Start Owning and Changing

THIRD BASE: STEP #1
Stop Blaming, Start Owning & Changing
What Is Your Responsibility?

Amy, 18 years old, sat in my counselling office. She said a speech that sounded all too familiar: "My parents don't love me. They're upset because I moved out and I've practically dropped out of school. My sister does nothing but nag at me. I can't stand being there. My teachers are after me because I hardly ever go to school . . . ." And she went on and on. She blamed everyone but herself. Finally I said, "Amy, **stop** for a second. I've heard that your sister, mother, father, teachers, friends and everyone else in your physical environment are at fault for your life. So what is your fault? What is your responsibility in all of this?" She looked puzzled and stunned. "My responsibility? I don't know. I know I'm not perfect, but it's all their fault." I tried to explain. "Amy, whenever there is a conflict, it's important for us to look at what our responsibilities are. How did you respond? What did you say? What did your body language communicate to your parents, siblings, friends and teachers? Are you telling me that you did NOTHING wrong? Especially in conflict, there are two sides to every story, and it's important that we look at and focus on ourselves. We can't change other people, but we can work on ourselves. So take a moment and review how you handled this conflict. Ask yourself what you learned about yourself."

Now Amy was completely speechless. This girl, who had talked non-stop since entering my room, could not say a word. I could tell she was **focussing** completely on the other people as being wrong to deflect the attention away from herself. That was her clever way, probably done unconsciously, of blaming and avoiding responsibility.

After 5 minutes (which seems like an eternity in a counselling room) she said, "OK, I learned that I can be selfish. I guess my parents were right when they told me that. I am selfish. All I think about really is myself. But I guess I thought that was OK because I'm a teenager. I learned that I can really lose it. I have a bad temper, and if someone knows how to **PUSH** my buttons, I will swear and attack them. And I learned that I guess I do have the habit of blaming other people. I never realised I did this before, but I guess I do it because it's really difficult focussing on my responsibility."

I couldn't believe it! Within only 5 minutes, Amy had matured by leaps and bounds! For the first time, she started owning what was her responsibility. I'm not saying that her friends', teachers', or siblings' behaviour was mature. But remember, we cannot control or change other people, only ourselves. So it only makes sense to focus first on ourselves, our response and attitude, and look at what needs to change.

How Will You Use This "Owning-Up" New Information? How Will Your Attitude and Behaviour Change?

Amy now had taken ownership. It's great to get to that level. But the difficult part is how this new information will impact your life. I asked Amy the following: "Now that you have shared with me what you have learned about yourself, how can you use this information to better who you are? How will you change?" At this point, she was totally stumped! AI have absolutely no idea," she replied. I **CONTINUED** to challenge her. "Amy, you've now admitted to me what your responsibility was in these various conflicts. What would be the very mature thing to do now?" She finally said, "But my parents and sister are not apologising. Why should I?" I challenged her that owning and apologising for her responsibility is absolutely the most mature thing to do. And it is possible for the teenager to be more mature than their parents at times. I know some adults who are NOT able or willing to apologise for their actions. But does that mean that we don't need to do it either? No! More importantly, apologising or "Owning-Up" for our own wrongdoing is really cleaning up our act. It shows ourselves and others that we are growing, learning and taking responsibility for our life.

I encouraged "my to talk with her parents, focussing only on what was her responsibility, not to blame or attack them, yet being careful not to over-apologise.

The following week seemed like a miracle! She came back to me, with a huge grin, and said, "Karyn, I confronted my parents. I apologised for my selfish behaviour and my bad attitude, and told them I really did love them. I realised that I do blame other people a lot. I didn't realise I did that so much. Anyway, both my parents started to cry and asked me to move back home. So, this past week, I moved out from my boyfriend's and back to my parents' house. I feel so GOOD about myself."

The neat aspect of this is that I was the coach and Amy was the player on the field. I challenged her old way of thinking and behaving, and she ran with the challenge, literally. The interesting part is that she STOPPED blaming others, focussed on her responsibility, and started owning and changing herself. The result? She said, "I felt so good about myself". We may think that we would feel worse, but in reality, we are growing and maturing when we do this. When we take action and admit our responsibility, this builds our self-esteem and maturity.

So, now I want to make you think. Think about the various areas of your life. Have you had any conflict in any of these areas during the last month? If so, think about what your responsibility was. **THINK** about how you acted. What did you say? How did you behave? What was your body language communicating? What did you learn about yourself? Now, record it all on the following pages.

STEP #1: Stop Blaming, Start Owning & Changing
EXERCISE

After thinking carefully about each of the various areas of your life shown on the chart below, honestly fill in answers to each of the two questions, in the second and third columns. This isn't easy to do, but the process in doing each question will make you much more **AWARE** and honest with yourself.

FOCUS ON THE FOLLOWING AREAS OF YOUR LIFE:

* List 1-3 conflicts you have experienced during the last month. * *Be specific.*

Friendships

Relationships

Parents

Brothers & Sisters

Part-time Job

School

Money

STOP BLAMING:

* What was your responsibility?
* What did you learn about yourself?
* What could you have done differently to improve the situation?

Friendships

Relationships

Parents

Brothers & Sisters

Part-time Job

School

Money

START OWNING:

* How will you use this information to better yourself?
* How will your attitude or behaviour change?

Friendships

Relationships

Parents

| |
| |

Brothers & Sisters

| |
| |

Part-time Job

| |
| |

School

| |
| |

Money

THIRD BASE: STEP #2
Crank & Change the Tunes
A LOOK AT EXTERNAL INFLUENCES

* Crank the Tunes!
* Know your influences: Music/Friends/Media/
  Relationships/Other.
* Are these influences pulling you up or weighing you down?
* Change the Tunes!
* Choose POSITIVE influences.

STATISTICS

* A national American study, looking at self-esteem,
  showed that teens involved in religious groups
  evaluated themselves more positively than
  teens not participating in a church youth group.[lvii]

About 1 year ago, I spoke to a high school assembly. Afterwards, a girl of around 16 years of age came up to me. Many teachers probably VIEWED this girl as "messed up" since she appeared as a Goth, black coat, tons of body piercing, tattoos and a white powdered face. Inside, this girl was a sweetheart, with a really sweet disposition, but extremely depressed and confused. She said to me, "Karyn, I started slitting my wrists last night. I hate myself. I wanted to die." She reached out her hands and showed me the marks on her wrists–they were still bruised and red. I asked her, "What made you **STOP**?" She said, "I had heard that some girl [me] was coming to talk to us today about self-esteem. I thought I should hear what she said before I really did it."

I talked with her for almost 30 minutes. I asked her, "What is happening in your life right now that is making you feel depressed?" Very quickly she said, "I have no control of my life! My parents dictate everything to me!" I challenged her, asking, "Do you have control of your attitude?" She replied, "Yes!" I continued, "Do you have control of your behaviour?" She replied, "Well, yes." I could see her getting slightly defensive. I said, "You're right, you can't control or change your parents. But you CAN control how you respond to them. You can control how you live your life. You can control what you think and what you do." I didn't think she'd understood me. So I asked her, "Do you choose your music, friends, media, attitudes, behaviour?" She said, "Yes."

> Then I asked her the big question:
> "Be honest with yourself. Does your
> music lift you up or weigh you down?"

She didn't respond. I continued, "What music do you listen to most often?" She named a few different bands. I make it a habit never to tell anyone what they should or should not listen to. I feel music is a very personal choice. However, I did ask her, "When you listen to your music, how do you **FEEL**?" Quietly she said, "Depressed and angry." So I said, "Part of moving towards healthy self-esteem is to take action and control of our life, as well as setting goals for ourselves that will lift us up! If you're listening to music that is depressing, naturally you will feel depressed. What's one goal that you would like to set for yourself, one that will pull you up?" She actually suggested putting away some of her music and listening to more uplifting music. A week later, I was back at the school and talked with her. She said very honestly, "Karyn, I really didn't think changing my music style would **alter** my moods. But it actually did. My depression isn't over, but it's slightly better now. I feel I'm one step closer."

Change the Tunes!
Choose Positive Influences

She figured it out. It takes one step at a time. She was right. Just changing your music will not eliminate depression or give you positive self-esteem. But look at the bigger picture. It's not about music, friends or media. It's about this 16-year-old girl telling herself, "I'm **WORTH** it . . . . I'm going to look at my life and begin to change what doesn't lift me up. Even if I love it, I know it's not good for me. If it makes me feel bad about myself, it's gone. The bottom line is, I love myself more than these things and influences!"

For her, change meant listening to other music. For other teens, change may mean different things: changing their reading choices (e.g., fashion magazines that make them feel inadequate after reading them); spending less time with their parents because they're so negative and perhaps excessively faultfinding; getting rid of a negative boyfriend or girlfriend, although usually it takes more time for this to happen; LETTING go of negative friends, in hopes of finding more positive influences.

Change is difficult! I never said this section was going to be easy. Some of you might be able to change quickly. Others may take months before feeling ready to change. Just keep asking yourself, "Is this (influence), lifting me up or weighing me down? Or, does this (influence) encourage or discourage me?" This is a key question!

Like this 16-year-old girl, we **OFTEN** think we have no control. Things just happen to us, and we are only helpless by-products of life's circumstances. But as I mentioned earlier, we have more control than we realise! We control our attitudes and behaviour. So, what's left? Not much! Remember the serenity prayer I mentioned before:

> God, grant me the serenity to accept the
> things I cannot change,
> courage to change the things I can,
> and the wisdom to know the difference.

I **CHALLENGE** you to look at the influences in your life: music, media, friends, boyfriends/girlfriends, family, etc. Be honest with yourself! Do these influences lift you up or pull you down? Ask yourself, "What do I want to **change**?"

Some want to modify their music tastes to more uplifting music. Other teens "get rid" of deadweight friends or relationship partners. Parents can be difficult at times, and we may not be able to change them . . . but again look at your part of the conflict and do some soul-searching. (See Step #1.) I do think it's important to have positive parental influences. So, if your parents are not encouraging, start hanging out occasionally with other adults who do lift you up (e.g., your friend's parents). Again, that is you making a positive choice to change your circumstances.

Some of these changes come at a high cost. I shared earlier that part of my journey towards being a Lifer was to let go of my Disguised friends and look for the Lifer friends. This was not easy, and it was a process, but the rewards, short and long-term, were great! I developed some real long-lasting friendships, and I surrounded myself with positive influences!

STEP #2: Crank & Change the Tunes EXERCISE

Take Action! List past and/or current influences.

● Be Specific! ● Does this influence pull you up or weigh you down? Be honest with yourself! If this is a past influence, what can you learn about yourself? ● Why did you "let go" of this influence?

● If this is a current influence, what do you want to change, if anything, about this influence?

Closest Friends

1._____

2._____

3._____

4._____

5._____

Past and Current Relationship Partners

1. _____

2. _____

3. _____

4. _____

5. _____

Favourite Magazines

1. _____

2. _____

3. _____

4. _____

5. _____

Close Family & Relatives

1. _____

2. _____

3. _____

4._____

5._____

Favourite Music Groups

1._____

2._____

3._____

4._____

5._____

Favourite TV Shows

1._____

2._____

3._____

4._____

5._____

Favourite Internet Sites

1._____

2._____

3._____

4._____

5._____

Other Influences

1._____

2._____

3._____

4._____

5._____

THIRD BASE: STEP #3
Chuck Blinders & Seek Strengths

* Remember: We all have strengths; we just may not know what they are!
* Using Your **HEAD**, not so much your heart, focus on your strengths!
* Where do you belong?
* Who values and loves you?
* What are your abilities and gifts? Check out the list.
* **Selective Attention:** Listen for your strengths!
* Add to and read your strengths daily!

STATISTICS

* When 60 youth with low self-esteem were instructed to read 15 self-statements to themselves 3 times a day for 2 weeks (these statements were negative comments restated positively), the results showed significantly increased scores of self-esteem and decreased depression.[lviii]

Increase Your Value

Often when I ask teens to identify their strengths, I hear, "I don't have any strengths." And I'll respond, "It sounds like you don't feel as if you have any strengths, but is that the truth? If I were to ask your family and friends, would they agree with you? Probably not!" I always challenge this "negative belief" because I firmly disagree with it! I have worked with hundreds of teens and have NEVER found one without strengths. Personally, I feel very strongly that we all are created with gifts! But the problem is that the Blind and Disguised often devalue their "strengths."

Have you ever tried giving a compliment to someone and he/she responds in one of the following ways? "You're just saying that." "Oh, that's no big deal. Anyone can do that." "You're my friend (or my parent). You have to say nice things." As the compliment giver, you can find it frustrating because the person minimises and devalues their strengths. Often, the compliment giver will stop giving the compliments because they're tired of hearing the negative reaction. Giving negative reactions is a habit that needs to be broken!

Start to increase the value of your strengths, and remember that you have the choice of how valuable a strength really is. One Disguised teen I counselled had a beautiful smile. When I asked him for his strengths, he couldn't think of any. So I began complimenting him on some of his strong character traits that I'd noticed, one being his beautiful smile. However, his previous habit kicked in, making him say, "Karyn, it's no big deal. **EVERYONE** smiles." But I disagreed with him. I've worked with people who rarely smile; let me tell you, it impacts upon the whole mood of any conversation. I feel as though I'm walking on eggshells when someone looks depressed or sad most of the time. I feel uncomfortable because I'm thinking they don't really want to be talking with me. So I really appreciate a friendly smile, and therefore to me smiling is a **strength**. It has value. The young client devalued his smile and thus didn't even think of it as a strength.

Another Blind teen struggled with a similar worldview. She had an excellent telephone voice and manners, which I noticed and shared with her. She responded, "Big deal." But I challenged her that having a positive telephone voice *is* a big deal! When someone calls at her work, she is the first person who gives the caller an impression of the company. If a receptionist is cranky or crusty, her telephone manners can drive customers away! I **know** for myself that when I get an irritated salesperson on the phone, I get easily turned off and call elsewhere. This teen devalued one of her strengths.

When we make devaluing comments, it's harmful for two reasons. First of all, it **ELIMINATES** that strength from your list. By saying, "It's no big deal," you're cheating yourself by not acknowledging what really is a big deal. Second, it's a put-down to the person who gave the compliment. If I say that smiling and pleasant telephone manners are important to me (which is true), and someone responds saying, "It's no big deal," they are now devaluing my opinion. To me, those strengths are important, and nobody can make me believe otherwise.

To **break** the habit of negating strengths, take these devaluing comments out of your vocabulary:

> "It's no big deal."
> "Anyone can do that."
> "That's nothing special."
> "Who cares?"
> "You're (They're) just saying that."
> "Whatever."
> "So what?"

Try CHANGING your thinking to

> "It is a big deal!"
> "It's important enough that someone else noticed and mentioned it."
> "It is a strength."
> "It is important and does have value."
> "Nobody (not even a parent or a friend) needs to give positive compliments. So I will listen to what they have to say about my strengths."

Often the Blind and Disguised may **_KNOW_** that they have strengths, but they don't _feel_ as if those strengths are valuable! They have relied on their heart, not their head, to determine what is truth, and that can be dangerous. The heart can be deceiving, but the head speaks truth. Feelings go up and down like a yo-yo. Most of us have days when we feel "unattractive," "blah" or "boring," but are we? Nope, the truth is we've just had a discouraging day or event! We must listen to what our head is telling us.

I strongly believe that when our heads and hearts give different messages, we should rely on our head. It's safer! But I find that we're making a good decision when our head and heart are saying similar things. Imagine that I feel tired or don't want to go to work. If I rely on my heart, I will lose my job. However, I **listen** to my head's messages to guide my decision-making: "Karyn, you have made a commitment to this job; people are relying on you."

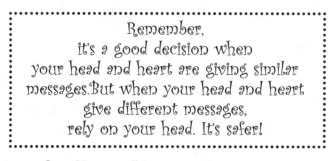

Remember,
it's a good decision when
your head and heart are giving similar
messages. But when your head and heart
give different messages,
rely on your head. It's safer!

Focus On Your Strengths

Try brainstorming your strengths! WRITE down as many as you can before looking at the lists below. How many did you get? I'll give you some help by providing various strengths that other teens have shared with me.

If you feel comfortable, ask one or two close friends or family members to help you brainstorm some of your strengths, but don't show them your list. So often, the people around us appreciate and value qualities about us that we do not notice, but which nonetheless are important and valuable.

STEP #3: Chuck Blinders & Seek Strengths
EXERCISE

1) Where do you BELONG?

List all the places where you feel connected and part of a group (e.g., school, home, youth group, sports team, a friend's home).

_____

_____

_____

_____

_____

_____

_____

_____

_____

_____

_____

_____

_____

_____

2) Who VALUES and loves you?

- **List** all your family members, relatives and friends who care about you.
- **Circle** the top five people who encourage, support and challenge you. These five people represent your "root" support system.

- How much time per week/month do you spend with these people?
- Would you like to spend more time with them? What can you do about this?

_____

_____

_____

_____

_____

_____

_____

_____

_____

_____

_____

3) What are your GIFTS?

Describe your character.

List all your character traits, abilities and gifts.

Check the list below to help generate more ideas.

_____

_____

_____

_____

_____

_____

_____

_____

What inner traits describe you?
What are you made of?
What have others told you about yourself?

☐ affectionate	☐ loving	☐ loyal
☐ generous	☐ carefree	☐ persistent
☐ focussed	☐ passionate	☐ adventurous
☐ risk taker	☐ giving	☐ compassionate
☐ responsible	☐ affirming	☐ accepting
☐ friendly	☐ self-motivated	☐ relaxed
☐ sociable	☐ accepting	☐ courageous
☐ determined	☐ positive	☐ disciplined
☐ encouraging	☐ artistic	☐ modest
☐ calm	☐ excited	☐ honest
☐ assertive	☐ easygoing	☐ diligent
☐ hardworking	☐ sensitive	☐ respectful
☐ careful	☐ strong listener	☐ visionary
☐ leader	☐ persuasive	☐ creative
☐ polite	☐ helpful	☐ ambitious
☐ funny	☐ understanding	☐ reliable
☐ patient	☐ sincere	☐ detail oriented

Inner traits often affect the gifts we develop. What gifts have you developed?

- ☐ good musician (piano, drums, singer, songwriter, etc.)

- ☐ good athlete (soccer, volleyball, basketball, field hockey, swimming, etc.)

- ☐ works hard at school (math, science, art, history, sociology, etc.)

- ☐ likes to take risks and try new things

- ☐ likes public speaking

- ☐ focuses on others

- ☐ contributes to society (giving to others)

- ☐ helps friends in need

- ☐ includes other people

- ☐ sociable

- ☐ a good friend

- ☐ kind to your parents

- ☐ responsible with your homework

- ☐ good with money management

This is not an exhaustive list, but rather it is meant to help you generate your own list.

Selective Attention: Listen For Your Strengths

Now that you have taken action and have started building up a list of strengths, it's important to hear and think about the positive comments from others. Let me ask you a silly question. How many red cars have you seen this week? Five? Ten? Don't know? You probably won't be able to tell me the exact number because you weren't looking for them. But if I'd asked you to **count** every red car you saw this week, your attention would have been heightened, and chances are you would have given a more accurate number.

So what is with the silly question? We hear and see what we already believe, whatever is on our self-esteem blueprint. Yet we all have selective attention. We tune in and out of stimuli around us. We all do this because there are so many stimuli in the world. Yet this selective attention also applies to our self-esteem. If I feel bad about myself, I will hear negative comments and probably fail to take in positive things said. As with the red cars, if we're not specifically looking for positive comments, we often will fail to see or hear them. Continue to brainstorm your strengths and start *looking and listening for any kind of positive comment.*

Add To and Read Your Strengths Daily

Don't be discouraged if you still don't **_FEEL_** as if your strengths are true. Remember–think first with your head and then feel with your heart. The more you hear positive comments and build your strengths list, the more your head will almost start convincing your heart. One exercise that teens have shared that is helpful is to read their list of strengths from 1 to 5 times daily. One teenaged girl I counselled said this to me:

> "Karyn, at first I would just write down any strength. My head and heart didn't buy into this list. I thought this was a waste of time. But over time I tried to build my list. I tried to write down strengths when I thought of them. I started hearing my friends compliment me. They probably did it before but I never heard it. My list has now continued to grow and I am slowly starting to believe and feel the difference."

The strengths list is not a onetime exercise. It's a lifetime exercise, where we continue to add to our list.

THIRD BASE: STEP #4
Turn Up the Truth & Turn Off the Lies

* The brain is like a tape player
* Empty your brain
* Filter and erase negative thoughts
* Control the record button
* Change negative thoughts to positive thoughts
* Build up your positive tape and SEARCH for the truth!

If there is one area that I spend a lot of time discussing with teens . . . this is it! I hear negative comments all the time from the Blind and Disguised: "I'm fat," "Nobody likes me," "I'm not going to do anything with my life," "I'll never pass," . . . . Especially with the Blind, negative comments pour out of their mouths. Just like any other habit, we fall into the rut of focussing on the negative and not the positive. The glass is seen as always half empty instead of half full.

The Brain Is Like a Tape Player

I see our brain as a tape player that holds two tapes, one negative and the other positive. When we hear an external negative message, the message comes through our tape deck (our brain), and quickly gets recorded on our negative tape. But often we don't even filter or screen what we record. We just hear a nasty comment and **record** it. Similarly, when we hear a positive comment, it comes through the tape deck and gets recorded on the positive tape.

The pattern with many Blind and Disguised is that their negative tape is completely full. If their positive tape has any messages on it, they rarely listen to it. Instead, the Blind and Disguised will often press the *replay* button on the negative tape, to listen to the negative messages over and over again. Obviously, you can imagine how these negative messages affect one's self-esteem.

Try completing the "Empty Your Brain" exercise. Be honest with yourself. What positive and negative comments do you tell yourself?

177

STEP #4A: Empty Your Brain
EXERCISE

Write out all the positive messages you have
memorised about yourself.

Write out all the **NEGATIVE** messages you have memorised about yourself.

STEP #4B: Filter Negative Thoughts EXERCISE

If you found it difficult filling out the positive side, you're not alone. Usually I see the negative side filled out first, and it is two or three times longer than the positive side. Now that you know what you're telling yourself, let's **CHALLENGE** those negative thoughts and create a filter. It's amazing how many of us listen to negative messages and automatically record these messages in our brain. Then, when we're feeling "crappy" about ourselves, we listen to that negative tape. We need a filter, because many of these negative messages are not truthful. If you hang out with many Disguised friends, chances are you have memorised many negative and untrue messages.

Use the following list of statements as a beginning *filter*. Look at your list and cross out any of your negative thoughts if the following statements apply to them. The examples I provide below are actually from teens.

ERASE The Negative Thought if . . .

(1) You <u>know</u>, deep down, it's untrue, but you tell it to yourself anyway.
(For example, "I'm fat, even though I weigh 120 pounds.")

For this first filter, listen to your head, not your heart. It's amazing how many people I talk with <u>know</u> that their negative messages are lies, yet, because they <u>feel</u> they are true, they tell themselves these lies anyway. One anorexic teen told me, "I know I'm not fat, but I feel I'm fat."

The Third-Party Truth

One trick to figuring out the "truth" is putting yourself in the position of a third party. Imagine that you tell yourself regularly that you feel fat because you weigh 120 pounds. You have a best friend who is **EXACTLY** like you. She looks, sounds, talks and weighs the same as you. She tells you that she feels fat. Would you agree with her? Remember, this friend means the world to you. You love her so much and want the best for her! Would you tell her to go on a diet, to starve herself? Would you make nasty comments, such as "Well, you are fat." No? Why not? Are those not the comments you tell yourself? Or would you say, "You look healthy and beautiful. Your weight is healthy for your body shape. I love you just the way you are!" Are these statements lies? Do you really **BELIEVE** these positive statements? Most of us speak truth to our friends because we're able to be a little more objective. We're speaking out of the head, and not the heart as much. So if you're not lying to your friend, it seems that you're lying to yourself.

Many of us give positive comments to our friends because we want them to feel great about themselves. However, let's start listening to these positive statements for ourselves!

Personally, I trust someone's opinion a lot more if I know they actually believe for themselves what they are telling me. Let's not be hypocrites. Let's live what we preach to our friends!

<u>ERASE</u> The Negative Thought if . . .

(2) It was told to you by someone <u>not</u> important to you.
(For example, a school bully has put you down.)

Remember that the Disguised often want to tear you apart. They may feel threatened or even jealous of you and want to control you. They want to "**push** your buttons" and get you upset. But don't just believe or record their comments in your mind. Why should their opinion matter when all they want to do is hurt you? Tell yourself that their opinion doesn't matter to you. The Disguised in your life can be bullies, former friends or sometimes even teachers and parents.

ERASE The Negative Thought if . . .

(3) It is an absolute statement.
"I'm ALWAYS stupid."
"You'll NEVER get a date."

Although we may feel stupid at times, it doesn't mean we are stupid. Besides, nobody is always stupid! These absolute statements, using the word "always" or "never," are untrue because very few circumstances happen always or never in life. It's true that **OCCASIONALLY** we may feel stupid if we answer an obvious question incorrectly, but this doesn't mean that we are stupid. It just means that we answered a question wrong. Change the words "never" and "always" to "sometimes" and "occasionally." Get rid of these absolute statements because they just make us feel worse and they are not true.

ERASE The Negative Thought if . . .

(4) It can be restated positively.
"I don't have any friends" can be restated to "I have many acquaintances. People like me. I just don't let them get too close. But I'm going to make an effort."

Remember, try focussing on the glass half full. Try to see any situation in a positive light. As the above example shows, it's important to understand our responsibilities in any situation. The teenaged girl who wrote the above comment had the habit of blaming everyone else. She failed to see that she was pushing people away. *Restating* her negative message helped her to see that friendships are important to her. It is her choice how she responds to people. She chooses whether she wants to push people away or to make an effort to be friendly.

ERASE The Negative Thought if . . . .

(5) It can be turned into a positive goal.
"I'm always negative"
can be turned into "Every day I'm going to focus on three positive things in my life."

"I'm bad with my money"
can be turned into "I'm going to set aside a certain amount to save every week."

"I put other people down"
can be turned into "I'm going to say at least one positive thing to every person I talk with every day."

In my opinion, setting goals is the best way to build our self-esteem. When we set goals, we are taking control of our life. Instead of being a passive bystander, we are **EMPOWERING** ourselves to "make our life happen." Every time a negative message comes into your mind, ask yourself, "What is my responsibility here? How can I work on this? What's the solution?"

Control the Record Button and Search For the Truth

The habit of negative thinking, like any habit, is NOT easy to break. But it is possible, because you control the record button of your tape player!

I recently counselled 17-year-old Amanda who bluntly told me, "I don't have any friends. Nobody likes me. Nobody ever says anything positive about me." Yet I had met earlier with her parents, who told me they had given her many positive comments. But she would ignore or disbelieve them.

When I met with her, I learned that writing poetry was one of her **GIFTS** and passions. I encouraged her to get a journal and start keeping track of her thoughts as we worked together in counselling. Her first week's assignment was to listen to and write out all compliments she was given. It didn't matter if she believed them or not. She was to write them out. To her surprise, the following week she had over 20 comments written out. She said she'd started feeling a little better because for the first time she was starting to <u>see</u> the positives. This step was a baby step for her to move towards being a Lifer. What was the truth? These comments were probably frequently made to her, yet she <u>**chose**</u> not to pay attention to them. Now she was becoming aware of some positive comments and recording them on her tape.

Amanda continued to write down positive comments. At first she didn't believe them, but after she began reading her list 3 times a day, her head was started to convince her heart. She realised that if all these positive comments were coming in, there must be some truth to them.

CLAIM the truth, stop the lies, control that record button, filter any negative comments coming from the Disguised, and press **replay** on your positive tape.

THIRD BASE: STEP #5
Grip Your Passionate Goals

* Claim Your **TOP** 10 Gifts.
* Filter Your Top 10 Gifts.
* Check Out Former Strategies.
* Tips to BUILD Your Goals.
* Design Your 5-Step Solution Plan to Get a Grip.
* WRITE Out Your Life Story.

In my opinion, this Step #5 is the most important step. Setting realistic goals has so many benefits! First of all, it means we are taking action and ownership of our life. When we play the victim of life's circumstances, it chains us down. When we set goals, however, we are breaking our own chains and indirectly saying, "I'm not happy about this in my life, but I'm going to stop complaining about it and do something about it." Setting goals provides a sense of empowerment and stops the "poor me" attitude, often heard expressed by the Blind or Disguised. Another benefit is that when we set goals, as long as they are realistic, we often benefit from attaining them, which provides a sense of accomplishment. Overall, setting *realistic* goals builds our self-esteem. Instead of being passive bystanders, watching our life pass by, we become active participants and realise that we actually can impact on the direction of our life. If our life is a book of experiences, the Blind and Disguised often feel they are reading their life, chapter by chapter. Meanwhile, the Lifers realise that they can start writing their own chapters.

As I shared in the Goal Setting Chapter, I struggled in school. When I received my grade of 38% in English class, negative thinking FLOODED my mind: "My life is going to be a waste." "I'm so stupid." "I'm not even going to make it through high school." "I'd better forget any thoughts of going to university." I felt so horrible, frustrated and useless.

Yet, as I've shared numerous times in this book, we need to FOCUS on what we can control and accept what we cannot. I realised I could not control the fact that I had a learning disability. However, I could control how I responded to it. Getting extra help from teachers, studying more regularly, and finding a tutor greatly helped me academically but more importantly emotionally. Academically, I watched my average slowly climb from 63% (in Grade 9) to 84% (in Grade 13). Interestingly enough, watching my average rise was the secondary blessing of my goal. Emotionally I learned that I could have an **impact** on my life, and this understanding was the beginning of a new self-esteem. I felt empowered and excited about what was to come. No longer did I have to play the victim. From now on, I was going to start setting goals in every area of my life, taking action to build my self-esteem and watching my life unfold.

When I was in Grade 9, I thought setting goals was boring, far too "mature," and had something to do with school. But I was wrong. Now I see that setting goals is like carving out a path. They don't need to be rigid, and I don't have to stick to that path, but it does provide guidance and direction. Goals can be about the character or skills we want to develop that are important to us. We can set personal goals, such as being more assertive or kind, or improving our friendships and relationships. Or we can set accomplishing goals, such as building friendships, travelling, managing money, improving grades, or going to college. Just ask yourself, if you were to write a book on your life, how would **YOU** like your life to unfold?

When I was 14 years old I did that. I told myself I wanted to be more assertive, choose good friends, work on improving my school average, become involved in two or three extra-curricular activities, and work on my shyness. Every day, I set small goals to help me work towards bigger goals.

The  ABCs of Goal Setting

Think of goals as being like the progression of the "A B C's." If A is where we are (e.g., shy) and C is where we want to go (e.g., outgoing), we need to work on B, the PROCESS or baby steps for getting from A to C. Many of us get stuck by only dreaming and talking about the "C's" we want for our life. We dream and dream and dream. Our friends and family may start to doubt our ability to ever get to C, because we talk much and act little. So when we come up with another "great idea," they may ignore us completely or try to look positive while deep inside doubting that we will do anything about it. **We** may even start doubting that we'll attain our C's. This self-doubt can be paralysing.

Once we know what we want (C), we need to set SMALLER, daily goals to achieve the larger goal (B) and actually take the risk and work towards the smaller goals.

When I was in Grade 9, I knew I was shy (A) and wanted to be more sociable (C). The tough part was thinking about how I was going to achieve that goal (B). I knew this big goal (C) would be a process and would take time, but I was willing to make the effort.

So in Grade 9 I started **ANALYSING** people who were outgoing. I studied their body language, tone of voice, gestures. One quality I noticed was that outgoing people usually give direct eye contact to the person to whom they are talking. This would be my first baby goal (B). So for one week I worked on looking people straight in the eye when talking with them. The second week, I would look at them and smile. The third week, I would look, smile and say their name. The fourth week, I would approach people instead of waiting for them to come to me. The plan was working, and I felt I was coming out of my shell. Grade 11 rolled around, and I was confronted with the largest goal I had ever faced.

Our school was very big into fashion shows! If you were part of this annual fashion show, you were an important part of the school. I was asked to be one of two commentators for the show. I had never done any public speaking up to this point. But SPEAKING was one of my goals to try. So I thought, why not?

That night turned out to be full of embarrassing moments! I had gone to get my makeup done. What a nightmare! They'd glued on these huge eyelashes, one inch in length, onto my eyelids. They were far too long and very heavy on my eyes. They were extremely uncomfortable. Then there was my dress, a big, pouffed, off-the-shoulder, long evening gown with lots of crinoline. Because the dress was off-the-shoulder, I **couldn't** wear a bra underneath.

Well, the night started! I was told only five hundred people would be coming. But that night, it was a sold-out house with over two thousand people. I was petrified! I kept thinking to myself, what have I got myself into? The music started, so Paul, the other commentator, and I walked out. I was SHOCKED to see that I had to climb up onto a two-foot-high platform to reach the microphone. There were no steps. So in between all 12 sets of the fashion show, Paul and I climbed up onto this platform. Of course it was a little more difficult for me because I was wearing this huge pouffed dress.

Within **15** minutes of the start of the show, as Paul and I said our lines, I noticed that the spotlights, which were extremely hot, had started melting the glue of my eyelashes. My eyes started to twitch, not only from the weight of these gigantic lashes, but now from the melted glue in them. I started to panic, and stuttered over my lines. Trying to stay calm, Paul told me to be in charge of door prizes. As I was starting to call out the door prize numbers, one of the false eyelashes flipped to a 90-degree angle, and then fell off and onto my notes. Paul **FREAKED** when he saw this huge lash on our paper. And now I had one eye with a huge lash and one without.

Now I was really frazzled. I kept trying to calm myself down. "Just do the door prizes. It's the easy job. Nothing can go wrong here," I kept thinking. I called out over 10 different numbers. Nobody was responding! I guess many people had lost or thrown out their tickets, unaware that prizes could be won. I was irritated, embarrassed and nervous. Finally, someone responded to one of the called-out numbers, but from up in the balcony. Without thinking, I said rudely, "Oh, get the prize later." People started to laugh. Apparently I'd sounded really bitchy. By this time, not only were my lashes melting, but I was MELTING! I would have preferred to be anywhere but there.

At last came intermission. I needed to cool down, breathe and pull myself together. I went to the change room and tried to put my eyelash back on. Of course, nobody had eyelash glue, and the other eyelash wouldn't come off. I got desperate and used Scotch-tape to keep the fallen lash on.

Before I knew it, it was back to the grind of the evening! I was not enjoying myself in the least. This night, which was a goal for myself, had turned into a nightmare.

Paul and I continued to climb up onto the platform to read our lines and off the platform when the fashion set was happening. After one of the sets, Paul and I stepped up onto the platform as usual. But as I grabbed my dress, my heel got caught in the front of my crinoline! So, as I stepped up, my shoe kept my dress down. Just as I stepped onto the platform, I realised that I was "flashing" my audience! There I was, bare-chested, wearing this ridiculous falling eyelash, in front of two thousand people! Was I mortified? Traumatised? I'm not sure if those two terms do justice to what I felt just then. For a 16-year-old, nothing could have been worse. I went home that night promising myself **NEVER** to do public speaking again. It was an absolute nightmare.

As I look back, I have mixed feelings about that night! Yes, it was my most embarrassing night ever! But, on the other hand, if I had not pushed myself to try something new, maybe I wouldn't be the public speaker I am now. Although I despised the humiliating situation, I had tried something new, which built me up, and surprisingly I had enjoyed the public speaking aspect of it. So I was able to see something positive in this incredibly disastrous event. Just because we set goals, and work towards them, it doesn't mean we are going to achieve them. However, just the fact we are TRYING something new is an accomplishment, and something to be proud of. If I had not taken the challenge of that speaking opportunity, maybe I would not be a public speaker now. We only learn what we like and don't like if we "take the risk." I frequently challenge teens telling them, "Get to know yourself! What are your dreams? What are your strengths? Grip them!" But how do you know what your gifts or strengths are if you don't try anything new?

As I look back now, some of the most difficult situations I faced were truly blessings in disguise. Today I am **thankful** that I struggled through high school, that I learned how to deal with my learning disability, because through it all, I learned several valuable lessons. Three years ago I went out with my dear friend Loreli, who summed it up so nicely. She was one of my best friends and got marks in the 80s to 90s without studying. Very honestly she said to me, "Karyn, if I were to do my life over again, I wish I would have to do it your way." I stopped her. "There's no way, Loreli, you would wish to struggle the way I did." She continued, "Yes, I would. You struggled. I didn't. To me, everything came too easily–friends, marks, sports. But, as a result, I didn't really learn about myself. I didn't know who I was. I had no motivation or self-discipline. But you, if you wanted something, you had to work for it. You learned time management, motivation, self-discipline, goal setting. Look where you are today. Your curse was your **BLESSING.**"

I'll never forget that conversation.

Setting realistic goals and achieving them is an art. It takes lots of practice, but is very worthwhile! I gained confidence in my goal setting throughout high school, so, by the time I was done, I knew who I was, what I wanted and where I wanted to go. After completing 6 years of post-secondary education, I started designing creative workshops for teens, specifically around the issue of self-esteem. These small workshops turned into high school assemblies and eventually into an international weekly TV show. Through working and speaking to thousands of teens, I've realised that many teens are dealing with the same stuff I faced.

When we set goals for ourselves, we take action and ownership of our life, and begin writing our own life story. So how do you want your life to **unfold**? First, start by claiming your goals and passions. What excites you? What kind of person do you want to become? What skills do you want to develop? What career **EXCITES** you and makes your heart pound? You'll probably find that this list will expand and change, and that's OK. We change as we grow older so naturally our list will change too. Just keep being aware of what you want!

> When we set goals for ourselves,
> we take action and
> ownership of our life,
> and begin writing our own life story.

STEP #5A: Claim Your Top 10 Goals EXERCISE

What kinds of things do you love to do?
What excites you and makes
your heart pound?
What kinds of activities energize you?

(A) **Brainstorm Your Goals**

What are personal goals that you want to develop?
What character traits do you want to **develop**?
What do you want to accomplish?

1._____

2._____

3._____

4._____

5._____

6._____

7._____

8._____

9._____

10._____

(B) **Now prioritize them, from your favourite to your least favourite.** Ask yourself, "How much time and ENERGY am I devoting to my goal?"
If you're not giving your goals the needed attention, what's holding you back?

I asked myself these questions when I was 15 years old, only to discover that travelling was one of my top 10 passions. Yet I had done barely any travelling. I knew what I wanted. Now I needed a plan of how to attain my passion. I made some calls and learned that for me to travel to Europe would cost roughly $1000.00. So I found myself a job working at a drugstore making $6.00/hour and started to save for my trip to Europe. I put myself on a tight budget, saving 50% and spending 50%. The following year I travelled to Germany, France and England. It was the trip of a lifetime and well worth it because I'd earned it. I **ACHIEVED** my goal of travelling by having a clear plan, applying tight discipline and expending lots of time and effort. This high school passion has turned into a lifestyle choice. Even today, I have a separate bank account for my "travel fund," and every month I put a certain percentage of my salary aside. Since travelling is one of my passions, my goal is to visit 30 countries by the time I am 30. By age 19, I was one third of my way towards my goal.

I'm amazed at how many of us have goals that COLLECT dust. We dream about them, but never get around to pursuing them. Remember, start writing the pages of your own book of life. What passions do you want to pursue? Which ones are the most reachable? Which ones are the most difficult to realise? I always recommend starting with the easy ones first. It builds confidence in our goal-setting ability for realising other passions. Before you design a clear plan of how to attain your passionate goal, filter through some of your passions first and list them.

STEP #5B: Filter Your Top 10 Goals EXERCISE

Try to Focus on
(1) goals that are yours, not your parents'

EXAMPLE: One teen told me, "I should love skating. I've done it all my life. My parents say I should love it because I'm so good at it, but I hate it." Part of building your self-esteem is really getting to know who you are, outside of your parents' views of you. Only you know what you really like. Nobody can tell you differently. Just be careful to really think for yourself. Sometimes I meet teens who want the exact opposite from what their parents want, for example, not to go to college, to prove to their parents that they themselves are in control. However, deep down they do want to go to college. What they fail to realise is that they are still being controlled, but in the opposite way. If you really want to go to college, go to college, even if its what your controlling parents want for you, too.

(2) goals that you have control over

EXAMPLE: The passion, "I want to be a rock star," is not necessarily in your control. It would be a more realistic goal to say, "I want to develop my musical ability and make a CD." That you do have control of.

195

(3) goals that are not image oriented

EXAMPLE: The goal, "I want to look really good," is again focussing on the outside appearance, and it's vague. It's better to focus on eating healthy and exercising.

(4) goals that are clear. Avoid vague goals.

EXAMPLE: The goals to "have fun" and "go places" are very vague. What is fun for you? What places do you want to go to? Be specific! It makes the plan much clearer to follow.

NOTE: The above examples were given to me by teens. Now . . . design the plan to grip your goals!

STEP #5C: Former Strategies EXERCISE

THINK ABOUT YOUR PAST GOALS . . .

Record one goal you would like to achieve within the next 5 weeks. Have you aimed for it in the past?

What feelings did you have about trying to achieve this goal? (e.g., fear, anxiety, stress, lack of motivation, uncertainty)

| |
| |
| |

What did these feelings tell you about yourself? (e.g., that I fear failure)

What was your previous plan for achieving your goal?

What worked?

What didn't work?

What did you learn from this past experience that will help you in your new solution plan?

STEP #5D: Techniques to Help You Achieve Your Goals
EXERCISE

(1)   Clarify your goals. Be as specific as you can.

(2)   Make them realistic.

(3)   Look at your own progress only. Try not to compare yourself with anyone else, unless this motivates you.

(4)   While focussing on your goals, don't forget to use your strengths.

(5)   Be accountable to someone. Let them know your goals.

(6)   Think about your constraints. What's holding you back?
   * fear of failure?   * fear of making a mistake?

   Are these obstacles and fears realistic?

(7)   Develop a 5-step solution plan (below) that works for you.
   * Imagine you've already achieved your goal.
   * What baby steps are needed to get there?
   * Set daily, weekly and monthly goals.

(8)   Measure your goal on a 0-10 scale, to evaluate your progress.
   * What was it that worked?
   * Was there anything you tried that didn't work?

Reward yourself!

STEP #5E: Design Your 5-Step Solution Plan To Grip Your Goals
EXERCISE

WHAT (C, from the ABCs of Goal Setting)

* What is your **passion**? What is your goal?

* Where are you now? If 10 means you have **ACHIEVED** your goal, and 0 means you haven't even tried, what number would you give yourself today?

* Where do you want to be in **5** weeks (on that scale of (0-10)?

HOW (B, from the ABCs of Goal Setting)

* How do you **PLAN** to achieve your goal? Imagine you've already achieved it. What was needed?
* Break your goal down into 5 weekly goals and the steps you need to achieve them.

WEEK 1   STEP #1

_____

_____

_____

WEEK 2   STEP #2

_____

_____

_____

WEEK 3   STEP #3

_____

_____

_____

WEEK 4   STEP #4

_____

_____

_____

_____

WEEK 5   STEP #5

_____

_____

_____

Cindy's story provides a good example of how to grip your passions.

Cindy wanted to "gain **confidence**." That was her goal. Yet it was vague. I went over these exercises with her. In the past, she'd never tried anything new. She wanted to gain confidence but didn't know how to go about it. So she'd never set it as a goal until she came to counselling.

I asked Cindy where her confidence was on that 0-10 scale (10 ' really confident and 0 ' no confidence). She gave herself a **3** on the confidence scale. I asked her, "In 5 weeks, what would be your realistic goal?" At first, she said her goal was to get it to 10 within 5 weeks. I reminded her to keep her goals realistic! Change takes time! So Cindy changed her goal to being at 6 on the confidence scale within 5 weeks.

Then we started working on "Cindy's 5 Steps Towards Gaining Confidence." I asked Cindy to imagine she was confident. How would life be DIFFERENT for her? How would her behaviour change? How would her thinking change? How would she and others know that she felt confident?
These were her 5 main answers.

(1) "Positive Body Language . . . .

If I were confident, I would keep my shoulders high and smile more."

(2) "Be assertive . . . .

If I were confident, I would share my thoughts and feelings with my friends. I would realise that my opinion was important."

(3) "I would try new things . . . .

I would go to a coffee shop by myself and feel OK. I would try new hairstyles, go to rock concerts, try windsurfing. I would try anything that's of interest to me because I wouldn't be afraid of failing."

(4) "More positive . . . .

I would start keeping a journal recording all the positives in my life instead of the negatives. I would give a compliment to 1 person each day."

(5) "Friendlier . . . .

I would say, 'Hi' to people and say their first name. I would try to go up to people instead of having people always coming up to me."

Cindy's 5-Step Plan was very specific. She knew exactly what needed to change for her to achieve her goal. Now she had her 5-Week Plan.

Cindy's 5-Week Plan

	WHAT	HOW OFTEN
First Week Goal	To improve body language: * smile more * shoulders up	* to smile 10 times a day regardless of whether she feels like smiling * to keep shoulders back 10 times a day regardless of how she feels about it
Second Week Goal	To be assertive * share thoughts and feelings	* to share once a day 1 thought or feeling with a friend, teacher or parent
Third Week Goal	To try new things * going to the mall alone * talking to new people	* to try 1 new thing once a week (e.g., talking with 1 person she hasn't talked to before)
Fourth Week Goal	To be more positive * listen for positives * to give more positives to others	* to listen every day for positives that people offer, and at the end of each day to write out all the positives in a journal * to give every day 1-3 positive compliments to people she cares about
Fifth Week Goal	To be friendlier * say "Hi, Susan." * go up to people	* to say "Hi (followed by the person's name)," while smiling, 3 times a day

The first week was the most difficult, but by week two, Cindy was doing the goals of both weeks one and two. By week five, Cindy was *completing* all the goals. And just as she'd hoped for, her confidence level shot up to **7** within 5 weeks, even higher than she'd predicted! She had taken action to boost her confidence. She felt better about herself, and her friends started noticing a difference!

Cindy would openly admit that it wasn't easy! But I never told her it would be easy! I just said that it was possible! It comes down to how motivated you are to achieve your goals.

It is easy to want goals. It's much tougher to make a plan, and actually work towards getting the goals. That is when we **NEED** lots of motivation and willpower. If you really want it, you've got to work on it. But, remember, every time you strive towards your goal, you are one step closer to becoming a Lifer. The rewards, as mentioned earlier, are endless and fabulous!

HOME PLATE

The Rewards

- **WHAT ARE THE REWARDS OF BEING A LIFER?**

ENJOY THE REWARDS OF CHOOSING TO HAVE A HEALTHY SELF-ESTEEM!

A recent study concluded that it is **NOT** money and popularity that make people the happiest! Shocked? Surprised? Most of us are since that is often what the media wants us to believe.

Rather, the "top four" of what makes people happy are a **healthy** self-esteem, knowing their abilities, having a sense of independence, and having friends/family with whom they connect.[lix]

I hope, by this point, you are starting to feel **empowered** and challenged! And I hope you're thinking, "Gee, this makes sense! This really is possible!"

I love working with youth at my counselling practice, and watching them feel empowered and act accordingly. I see them struggle at First Base, wondering if they are Blind, Disguised or a Lifer. I see many struggle to change their attitude. We spend weeks going over how their attitude has contaminated their life. What are the consequences? Then, the glorious day comes when they reach Third Base, when they say, "Karyn, I need to change. I want to be healthy. I want to be my own person. I'm ready to really work at this." Now they're ready to take action. They understand self-esteem is a huge deal and are willing to put some time and energy towards it! Slowly, change starts, confidence grows, esteem rises and, simultaneously, wonderful rewards come!

WHAT ARE THE INCREDIBLE REWARDS OF BEING A LIFER?
Overall, the Lifers . . .

* feel EQUAL to other people
* know their strengths, and work to strengthen or accept their weak areas
* feel they are unique, special and loved
* choose what to believe from others
* FILTER out negative comments
* learn from their mistakes
* take **RESPONSIBILITY** for themselves
* face life with confidence and happiness
* feel free to pursue any exciting challenge ahead

Specifically, the Lifers, in the area of...

Friendships
* are positive towards themselves and others
* usually choose other Lifer friends
* are not jealous of others' success

Body Language
* communicate equality
* smile frequently (real smiling–not fake)

* give pleasant facial expressions when talking
* give appropriate verbal feedback when listening
* feel comfortable with steady eye contact
* ask other people's opinion, showing they value others' opinions
* do not turn the conversation back to themselves, or try to control the conversation
* may disagree with others' opinions, but still respects them
* do not put others down
* keep shoulders straight and held high, communicating confidence
* hold head straight (but not too high), communicating security
* have arms and hands relaxed, communicating interest in what you are saying
* have voice **RELAXED**, coherent and confident

Relationships & Dating

* are attracted to other Lifers as partners
* don't need a relationship, but might want one
* feel like a whole person
* truly love themselves
* feel **content** to be either single or in a relationship
* have a "selfless love" towards their partners
* encourage and challenge their partners to strive for their goals and dreams
* have "Many Roots" and support systems
* strive to be interdependent (have friends outside the relationships)
* share similar interests with their partner but have their own personal interests

* have "together-time" with their partner and "personal-time"
* rely on their HEAD to make decisions, but listen to their heart
* learn about themselves from their experiences
* admit when they are wrong

Communication Style

* are assertive
* show interest in other people's ideas
* feel their opinions and thoughts are important
* feel confident **SHARING** their thoughts with others
* firmly and politely stand up for their opinions and feelings
* respect other people's viewpoints
* use "I" statements ("I feel frustrated when. . .")

Goal Setting

* set realistic goals, take risks and often achieve their goals
* make SMALL steps towards their realistic goals
* see crises as opportunities to be seized, or challenges to be met
* set external goals (e.g., trying out for a sports team) and internal goals (e.g., aiming to be kinder)
* compare their goals and improvements with reference to **THEMSELVES**, not others
* know what they want and set their own goals (not just what their parents or friends want)
* have confidence in their goal setting
* like trying new things

* aim to try their **BEST**
* are **not** afraid of failing, as long as they have tried their best
* set short and long-term goals

Self-Destructive Behaviours

* do not self-mutilate (they don't want to hurt themselves)
* want the best for themselves so eat HEALTHY (not starving or bingeing)
* set realistic goals, which they often achieve, and often feel in control of their life

Depression & Suicide

* sometimes feel depressed, but rarely do these feelings control them
* try to be assertive towards others with their thoughts and feelings
* **avoid** negative thinking and impulsive, irrational behaviour
* try to focus on their strengths
* work on or **ACCEPT** their weaknesses
* rarely go to a temporary "numb" state (not caring what happens to them)

Anger

* are ASSERTIVE with their anger
* listen carefully to the other person's concerns
* recognise that their anger is secondary to other emotions (hurt, sad frustrated)
* confront or level with the person whom they are angry (hurt, sad, frustrated) towards

* do NOT verbally attack or blame the other person for their feelings
* take ownership or admit their responsibility for their part in a conflict situation
* work out a plan of compromise with the other person(s)
* express their feelings of sadness, hurt and frustration through talking, art, poetry or sports
* express their feelings <u>not to change someone else</u>, but to stick up for themselves
* recognise their feelings are important
* are ready to apologise for their part in the disagreement

Body Image
* work towards the "**Inside-Out**"
* to maintain a healthy weight for themselves
* want to take care of their appearance, but not allow it to control them
* accept what they cannot change, and work on what they can change

Teens Whose Parents Divorced
* would feel sad and hurt that their parents have divorced
* would express their emotions
* understand that their parents' divorce is **not** their fault
* believe that they have two parents who care about them

Peer Pressure
* say "No" to what they don't want and "Yes" to what they do want

* do not encourage others to do or try something that they don't want to
* **respect** other people's decision of "No"

Abuse

* seek counselling and/or read material about the impact of the abuse on their self-esteem
* recognise that the abuse is not their fault
* **learn** to trust themselves and their intuition
* are assertive regarding verbally abusive comments (If someone said "You're stupid," the Lifer would reply, "Well, that's your opinion," or AI feel hurt when you say that.")
* **BREAK** the silence about the abuse and tell someone whom they **trust**
* try to avoid the abuser to protect themselves
* do not believe everything that the abuser says
* understand that they do have value, even though the abuser doesn't recognise that
* are attracted to friends and relationship partners who are kind, not abusive (e.g., the Blind)

Remember, I never said it was easy, but it is possible! Life is short, and too many of us, although physically alive, feel dead inside! I hope, by the time you're reading this section, you personally have reached Home Plate! I've talked a lot from **personal** experience in this book, because I wanted you to know that, although I'm a trained counsellor, I'm also human, and have personally struggled with the issue of self-esteem myself! It's often difficult to see the light at the end of the tunnel when we're Blind or Disguised. But it's my hope that this book will provide that light, to inspire you to keep going, give it all you have, keep trying. **You're** worth it. And if nobody in your whole life has told you that you are valuable, let me be the first. You <u>are</u> valuable! You are special! Every human being is unique, and we each deserve to feel appreciated and develop our gifts!

If self-esteem were a piece of white paper, who would be holding yours? For the Blind and Disguised, their peers and society are holding that paper. If their peers tell them they are worthless, it is written down on that paper and they believe it! But by this time, if you've really reached Home Plate, <u>you</u> are holding that piece of white paper called your **SELF-ESTEEM**. Only you can write anything on it. You CONTROL and own that piece of paper!I've said to many of my clients, "I am merely a coach, on the sidelines watching you play the game. I could be the best coach in the world, but no matter what, if you don't take the advice, nothing I do or say will matter. Only you can play that game, and it's up to you whether you want to listen to me or not. It's your GAME, and nobody can win it for you."

You've read the book, so now it's up to **YOU** to put it into play! It's your call. You know the game plan and have the skills to put everything into motion and be your absolute best. So go and write the life story that you want for yourself. You're the only author who's qualified to do the job. Make your life a BESTSELLER!

SPILL YOUR GUTS TO KARYN

Let her know what you thought about *Analyse Yourself*.
What did you **LEARN** about yourself? Your friends?
Your parents? Share your story! What was helpful?
Were you able to reach your goals? Send her an e-mail
describing your goals and the steps you took to reach them,
and how you did! Your ideas and work could be
featured in her next book!

If you have poetry, relevant to the various chapters,
send it in. Karyn encourages you to "express yourself" in
talking, **POETRY** and art.Your work may be
featured in an upcoming show or on her Web site.

Karyn works with youth in a variety of different ways,
including her TV show, high school workshops
and other creative opportunities.
If you would like to find more information about her
Youth Advisory Committee
or to schedule her to speak in your area,

email her at yacka@sympatico.ca.
or check out her website at

www.karyngordon.com

FOR FURTHER HELP

You may be feeling lost or hopeless. Remember, whatever
you are going through, you don't have to do it alone.
Call one of these resources.
They are all free and available to help you!

IN CANADA For any questions or help call
Kids Help Phone 1-800-668-6868.
This number is toll **free** across Canada, and confidential.

If you are attempting or thinking about suicide right now,
Call 9-1-1.

IN THE USA For **questions** related to substance abuse,
call the National Council on Alcoholism and
Drug Dependency Hopeline 1-800-NCA-CALL

If you or a friend is attempting or thinking about suicide
call the National Adolescent Suicide Hotline
1-800-621-4000

If you are attempting or thinking about suicide right now,
call 9-1-1. For questions related to eating disorders,
call the National **Youth** Crisis Hotline
1-800-448-4663

INDEX

WORKS CITED

Ballie, R. "Fifty-four percent of youth have tried an illicit drug." *Monitor on Psychology* 32 (5) June 2001.

Center for Disease Control. National Center for Injury Prevention and Control. <http://www.nosuicide.com>.

Coats, Erik J., Ronnie Janoff-Bulman, and Nancy Alpert. "Approach versus avoidance goals: Differences in self-evaluation and well-being." *Personality and Social Psychology Bulletin* 22 Oct. (10)(1996): 1057-1067.

DeSimone, Adrienne, Patricia Murray, and David Lester. "Alcohol use, self-esteem, depression, and suicidality in high school students." *Adolescence* 29 (1994): 939.

Driedger, Sharon Doyle. "Overcoming Depression." *Macleans Magazine* 12 Nov. 2000: 34-36.

Ebernathy, Thomas J, Lisa Massad, and Lisa Romano-Dwyer. "The relationship between smoking and self-esteem." *Adolescence* Win. 30(12)(1995): 899.

French, Simone A., Cheryl L. Perry, Gloria R. Leon, and Jayne A. Fulerson. "Changes in psychological variables and health behaviours by dieting status over a three-year period in a cohort of adolescent females." *Journal of Adolescent Health* 16 (6) June 1995: 438-447.

Giesler, R. Brian, Robert A. Josephs, and William B. Swann, Jr. "Self-verification in Clinical Depression: The Desire for Negative Evaluation." *Journal of Abnormal Psychology* 105 (3) Aug. 1996: 358-368.

Gordon, Karyn. "Dear Karyn." *What Magazine* Feb. 2001: 30.

Gordon, Karyn. "Dear Karyn." *What Magazine* June 2000: 60.

Gordon, Karyn. "Dear Karyn." *What Magazine* June 2001: 46.

Gordon, Karyn. "Dear Karyn." *What Magazine* Oct. 2000: 60.

Gowen, Kris. "Being teased by peers has a major impact on girls' body satisfaction." *American Psychological Association Online.* 17 August 1998: 1.

Harrison, J., J. Moller, and Stan Bordeaux. "Youth Suicide and Self-Injury in Australia." *Australian Injury Prevention Bulletin* 15 (Feb. 1997).

Hope, Jean T., Laurel L. Copeland, Ruth Maharg, and Ted E. Dielman. "Assessment of Adolescent Refusal Skills in Alcohol Misuse Prevention Study." *Health Education Quarterly* 20 (3) 1993: 373-390.

Janhevich, Derek. "Violence Committed by Strangers." *Juristat* 18 (9) June 1999: 9.

Kinnier, Richard T., Arlene T. Metha, Jeanmarie S. Keim, Jeffrey L. Okey, et al. "Depression, meaninglessness, and substance abuse in "normal" and hospitalized adolescents." *Journal of Alcohol and Drug Education* 39 (2) 1994: 101-111.

Langlois, Christine. "Teen Angst." *Parenting Magazine* April 1999: 76.

McCullough, P. Michael, Donna Ashbridge, and Rebecca Pegg. "The effect of self-esteem, family structure, locus of control, and career goals on adolescent leadership behaviour." *Adolescence* 29 (115) Fall 1994: 605-611.

Miserandino, Marianne. "Belief in one's abilities has more to do with success in school than natural ability." *American Psychological Association Online* Press Release 1996: 1.

Morris, Marika. "Violence against Women and Girls." Canadian Research Institute for the Advancement of Women (Fact Sheet). <http://www.ffq.qc.ca/marche2000>.

National Institute for Mental Health, suicide"rochford.org, 2001.

Overholser, James C., Dalia M. Adams, Kim L. Lehnert, and David C. Brinkman. "Self-esteem deficits and suicidal tendencies among adolescents." *Journal of the American Academy of Child and Adolescent Psychiatry* 34 (7) 1995: 919-928.

Partenheimer, David. "Study finds autonomy, competence, relatedness, and self-esteem at top of list of psychological needs." *American Psychological Association Online* 11 Feb. 2001: 1.

Peikin, David. "Boys and Girls Are Cruel to Each Other in Different Ways–But Effects Are Equally Harmful." *American Psychological Association Online* 25 March 1998: 1.

"People with Depression Tend to Seek Negative Feedback." *American Psychological Association Online* Press Release 1996: <http//www.apa.org>.

Philpot, Vincent D., and Jay W. Bamburg. "Rehearsal of positive self-statements and restructured negative self-statements in increased self-esteem and decreased depression." *Psychological Reports* 1 (29 Aug. 1996): 83-91.

Rabasca, L. "Psychotherapy may be as useful as drugs in treating depression, study suggests." *American Psychological Association* 30 (8) Sept. 1999: 1.

"Respecting and Understanding Body Image." <u>Statistics: Eating Disorders and Their Precursors</u>. <http://www.msu.edu/~rubi/2001>.

Satir, Virginia. *The New Peoplemaking*. Mountain View: Science and Behavior Books, 1988.

Statistics Canada—Family Violence in Canada. Ottawa: Ministry of Industry, 1999: 30.

Statistics Canada—National Health Survey. 1994/95 – 1998/99.

Statistics Canada. "Sex Offenders." *Juristat* 19 (3) March 1999.

"Teen Dating Violence" – Fact Sheet. <http://www.teenrelationships.org/statistics/stats.htm> 2001.

Trainor, Cathy. "Canada's Shelters for Abused Women." *Juristat* 19 (6)
    June 1999: 7.

"Warning Signs of Teen Violence: Reasons for Violence." American Psycho-
    logical Association Help Center—Brochure.
    <http://www.helping.apa.org> 2001.

Whitfield, David. "Increasing interest and achievement motivation among
    adolescents: An overview." *High School Journal* 79 (1) Oct.-Nov. 79:
    33-40.

Willenz, Pam. "Religious involvement found to have largest influence on
    self-esteem of young adolescents, according to national survey."
    American Psychological Association Online 24 Aug. 2001: 1.

"Women and Depression." *American Psychological Association Online* Brief-
    ing Sheet. <http://www.apa.org>.

ENDNOTES

[i] Virginia Satir, *The New Peoplemaking* (Mountain View: Science and Behavior Books, 1988) 22-24.

[ii] Satir 22.

[iii] R. Brian Giesler; Robert A. Josephs, and William B. Swann, Jr., "Self-verification in Clinical Depression: The Desire for Negative Evaluation." *Journal of Abnormal Psychology* 105 3 (Aug. 1996): 358-68.

[iv] David Peikin, "Boys and Girls Are Cruel to Each Other in Different Ways-But Effects Are Equally Harmful." American Psychological Association Online 25 March 1998: 1.

[v] Giesler, Josephs, and Swann 358-68.

[vi] Karyn Gordon. "Dear Karyn." *What Magazine* Oct. 2000: 60.

[vii] Erik J. Coats, Ronnie Janoff-Bulman, and NancyAlpert, "Approach versus avoidance goals: Differences in self-evaluation and well-being." *Personality and Social Psychology Bulletin* 22 Oct. (10)(1996):1057-1067.

[viii] P. Michael McCullough, Donna Ashbridge, and Rebecca Pegg, "The effect of self-esteem, family structure, locus of control, and career goals on adolescent leadership behaviour." *Adolescence* Fall 29 (115)(1994): 605-611.

[ix] David Whitfield, "Increasing interest and achievement motivation among adolescents: An overview,"_High School Journal_ Oct.-Nov. 79(1)(1995): 33-40.

[x] Marianne Miserandino, "Belief in one's abilities has more to do with success in school than natural ability," *American Psychological Association Online*, Press Release 1996: 1.

[xi] Christine Langlois, "Teen Angst," *Parenting Magazine*, April 1999: 76.

[xii] Adrienne DeSimone, Patricia Murray, and David Lester, "Alcohol use, self-esteem, depression, and suicidality in high school students," *Adolescence* 29 (1994): 939.

[xiii] Giesler, Josephs, and Swann 358-68.

[xiv] Richard T. Kinnier, Arlene T. Metha, Jeanmarie S. Keim, Jeffrey L. Okey, et al, "Depression, meaninglessness, and substance abuse in "normal" and hospitalized adolescents," *Journal of Alcohol and Drug Education* 39 (2) (1994): 101-111.

[xv] Simone A. French, Cheryl L. Perry, Gloria R. Leon, and Jayne A. Fulerson, "Changes in psychological variables and health behaviours by dieting status over a three-year period in a cohort of adolescent females," *Journal of Adolescent Health* 16 June (6)(1995): 438-447.

[xvi] Thomas J. Ebernathy, Lisa Massad, and Lisa Romano-Dwyer, "The relationship between smoking and self-esteem," *Adolescence* Win. 30(12)(1995): 899.

[xvii] J. Harrison, J. Moller, and Stan Bordeaux, "Youth Suicide and Self-Injury in Australia," *Australian Injury Prevention Bulletin*, Feb. 1997, Issue 15.

[xviii] R. Ballie, "Fifty-four percent of youth have tried an illicit drug," *Monitor on Psychology*, Vol. 32, No. 5, June 2001.

[xix] Ballie, Vol. 32, No.5.

[xx] Jean T. Hope, Laurel A. Copeland, Ruth Maharg, Ted E. Dielman, et al, "Assessment of adolescent refusal skills in an Alcohol Misuse Prevention Study,"_Health Education Quarterly 20(3) (1993): 373-390.

[xxi] Giesler, Josephs, and Swann 358-68.

[xxii] Thomas J. Ebernathy, Lisa Massad, and Lisa Romano-Dwyer 899.

[xxiii] Simone A. French, Cheryl L. Perry, Gloria R. Leon, and Jayne A. Fulerson 438-447.

[xxiv] James C. Overholser, Dalia M. Adams, Kim L. Lehnert, and David C. Brinkman, "Self-esteem deficits and suicidal tendencies among adolescents," *Journal of the American Academy of Child and Adolescent Psychiatry* 34(7) (1995): 919-928.

[xxv] *American Psychological Association Online*, "Women and Depression," Briefing sheet <http://www.apa.org>.

[xxvi] *American Psychological Association Online*, "People with Depression Tend to Seek Negative Feedback," 1996 Press Release <http//www.apa.org>.

[xxvii] Christine Langlois 76.

[xxviii] Statistics Canada, 1998.

[xxix] Centre for Disease Control, National Centre for Injury Prevention and Control; nosuicide.com; National Institute for Mental Health; suicide"rochford.org, 2001.

[xxx] Centre for Disease Control, National Centre for Injury Prevention and Control; nosuicide.com; National Institute for Mental Health; suicide"rochford.org, 2001.

[xxxi] J. Harrison, J. Moller, and Stan Bordeaux Feb. 1997, Issue 15.

[xxxii] Statistics Canada, National Health Survey, 1994/95-1998/99.

[xxxiii] Statistics Canada, National Health Survey, 1994/95-1998/99.

[xxxiv] Statistics Canada, 1998.

[xxxv] Centre for Disease Control, National Centre for Injury Prevention and Control; nosuicide.com; National Institute for Mental Health; suicide@rochford.org, 2001.

[xxxvi] Sharon Doyle Driedger, "Overcoming Depression," *Macleans Magazine*, 12 Nov.: 34-36.

[xxxvii] L. Rabasca, "Psychotherapy may be as useful as drugs in treating depression, study suggests," *American Psychological Association* (30)8, Sept. 1999: 1.

xxxviii Adrienne DeSimone, Patricia Murray, and David Lester 939

xxxix Karyn Gordon, "Dear Karyn," *What Magazine* June 2000: 60.

xl Karyn Gordon, "Dear Karyn," *What Magazine* June 2001: 46.

xli Kris Gowen, "Being teased by peers has a major impact on girls' body satisfaction," *American Psychological Association Online* 17 August 1998: 1.

xlii Respecting and Understanding Body Image, "Statistics: Eating Disorders and Their Precursors" <http://www.msu.edu/~rubi/2001>.

xliii Respecting and Understanding Body Image, "Statistics: Eating Disorders and Their Precursors" <http://www.msu.edu/~rubi/2001>.

xliv Respecting and Understanding Body Image, "Statistics: Eating Disorders and Their Precursors" <http://www.msu.edu/~rubi/2001>.

xlv Respecting and Understanding Body Image, "Statistics: Eating Disorders and Their Precursors" <http://www.msu.edu/~rubi/2001>.

xlvi Karyn Gordon,"Dear Karyn," *What Magazine* Feb. 2001: 30.

xlvii Statistics Canada, Family Violence in Canada (Ottawa: Ministry of Industry 1999) 30.

xlviii Statistics Canada, "Sex Offenders," *Juristat* (19) 3 March 1999.

xlix Cathy Trainor, "Canada's Shelters for Abused Women," *Juristat* (19) 6 June 1999: 7.

l Statistics Canada, *Family Violence in Canada* (Ottawa: Ministry of Industry, 1999).

li Marika Morris, "Violence against Women and Girls." Fact sheet for Canadian Research Institute for the Advancement of Women <http://www.ffq.qc.ca/marche 2000>.

lii Derek Janhevich, "Violence Committed by Strangers," *Juristat* (18) 9 June 1999: 9.

liii Fact sheet, "Teen Dating Violence" <http://www.teenrelationships.org/statistics/ stats.htm, 2001>.

liv Fact sheet, "Teen Dating Violence" <http://www.teenrelationships.org/statistics/ stats.htm, 2001>.

lv Fact sheet, "Teen Dating Violence" <http://www.teenrelationships.org/statistics/ stats.htm, 2001>.

lvi American Psychological Association Help Center, "Warning Signs of Teen Violence: Reasons for Violence," Brochure <http://www.helping.apa.org, 2001>.

lvii Pam Willenz, "Religious involvement found to have largest influence on self-esteem of young adolescents, according to national survey," *American Psychological Association Online* 24 Aug. 2001: 1.

lviii Vincent D. Philpot and Jay W. Bamburg, "Rehearsal of positive self-statements and restructured negative self-statements in increased self-esteem and decreased depression," *Psychological Reports* 29 Aug. (1)(1996): 83-91.

lix David Partenheimer, "Study finds autonomy, competence, relatedness, and self-esteem at top of list of psychological needs," *American Psychological Association Online* 11 Feb. 2001: 1.